GOOD OLD DAYS, MY ASS

GOOD OLD DAYS, MY ASS

665 Funny History Facts &
Terrifying Truths About Yesteryear

by David A. Fryxell

FAMILY
TREE
BOOKS

CINCINNATI, OHIO
shopfamilytree.com

CONTENTS

NOSTALGIA ISN'T WHAT IT USED TO BE

When the economy is in the dumps, wars rage on without end, partisanship reigns in politics, and you can't even catch a plane without having to take your shoes off to get through security, it's tempting to long for the "good old days." It's not just the headlines that make those halcyon days of yesteryear seem rosier: We have Bieber Fever, while they had Elvis. We pay an ever-escalating fortune to see a doctor for five brusque minutes, while back then, the friendly family physician made house calls. We sit fuming in commuter traffic, whereas in the good old days, the streetcars took you wherever you wanted to go while folks sang "Clang, clang, clang went the trolley."

Okay, maybe that last is a bit romanticized, but the Judy Garland movie about the 1904 World's Fair that gave us the trolley song, *Meet Me in St. Louis*, perfectly captures the idealized picture most of us have about the past. Back in those dreamy days gone by, our ancestors apparently had little more to worry about than which song to warble next while gathered in familial warmth around the piano. In the movie's world of the Smith family, the greatest crises arise over whether one daughter's boyfriend will finally get around to proposing and if Mr. Smith will move the family to New York, where he's gotten a better job. That would mean missing the fair! Even Katie the maid seems content, though she makes a mere twelve dollars a month.

The turn-of-the-century truth is a bit harsher. Those trolleys actually crawled along, despite the clanging of their bells, because good old-fashioned horse transportation wouldn't get out of their way. (The horses left behind smelly reminders of their passage—more than three million pounds a day in early-1900s New York City, where Mr. Smith wanted to relocate.) The gas lamps that give the world of *Meet Me in St. Louis* its warm glow were fountains of soot that left a grimy residue everywhere, blackened ceilings, corroded metal, and killed houseplants. They also had a nasty tendency to explode. Before the advent of meat inspection, there's no telling what was actually in the corned beef and cabbage that Katie the maid cooked up for the Smith family. Many of little daughter "Tootie" Smith's peers were working in cramped and dangerous mills and factories instead of enjoying an idyllic childhood; if child laborers got maimed for life, their parents might be paid one dollar in compensation.

Not to mention the prospect of spending summer in sultry St. Louis without air-conditioning.

But maybe the "good old days" weren't quite so long ago. Surely the middle of the twentieth century was a better time (if you can overlook the sixty million deaths in the Second World War) than these troubled first years of the twenty-first century? Another song nicely, if ironically, expresses our contemporary longing for *those* "good old days"—the theme from Norman Lear's TV sit-com, *All in the Family*:

"Boy, the way Glenn Miller played. Songs that made the hit parade. Guys like us, we had it made. Those were the days.

Didn't need no welfare state. Everybody pulled his weight.

Gee, our old LaSalle ran great. Those were the days.

And you know who you were then, girls were girls and men were men."

Of course, songwriters Lee Adams and Charles Strouse puncture Archie Bunker's gauzy reminiscence with the next line: "Mister, we could use a man like Herbert Hoover again." You mean the Herbert Hoover under whose presidency the Great Depression began? Well, maybe there were a few things wrong with the good old days, after all.

Indeed, when Archie was growing up in those "Hooverville" days, families like his were probably in bread lines. Even when the economy turned around, that old LaSalle had no airbags or seat belts, much less GPS navigation, and got less than ten miles a gallon; automotive fatality rates per mile were at least five times what they are today. "Girls were girls," but women had little opportunity to do anything besides be a housewife in a "man's world." The song goes on, "People seemed to be content. Fifty dollars paid the rent"—but back in 1944, when the United States' average rent was in fact fifty dollars, the average annual wage was just $2,400 a year. And even people's "contentment" was no doubt tempered by the constant fear of contracting polio, which peaked at 58,000 cases in the United States in 1952—before the Salk polio vaccine was introduced in 1955.

Few of us would really want to back to the "good old days" of polio and typhoid fever, child labor, and adulterated food, much less a world without air-conditioning, color television, computers, and the Internet. But it's easy to forget or gloss over just how rough our ancestors had it in those often-terrifying days of yesteryear.

The factoids and historical nuggets in this book aim to entertainingly remind readers how distorted our rose-tinted view of the past really is. While occasionally offering examples from ancient times, its focus is mostly on more recent "good old days," especially in America. Since most people are at least dimly aware of the big-picture shortcomings of life back when—world wars, slavery, mass slaughter, subjugation of indigenous peoples—this book emphasizes instead the day-to-day horrors and inconveniences of ordinary life. That's not to diminish the awfulness of wars and other atrocities, but rather to remind us that even when our forebears weren't killing or enslaving each other, life was no picnic. Just getting by from breakfast to bedtime was a challenge through most of human history. The "good old days" for most people were a filthy, dangerous, exhausting slog simply to survive.

Admittedly, that's not exactly the stuff of popular songs. But the next time you feel like griping about doffing your shoes in airline security, maybe it will help to remember that people haven't always *had* airplanes—and that the railroads whose era we romanticize were a rolling death trap that claimed more lives than some wars. Or, if you're frustrated about that long wait in your doctor's office, try passing the time by listing all the diseases you no longer have to worry about being diagnosed with. Even when it comes to entertainment, as you channel-surf for something diverting, keep in mind that for every Elvis and Glenn Miller they enjoyed back when, there were also flea circuses and theater fires. Our ancestors would have been thrilled at the chance to choose from five hundred channels, even with "nothing" on.

So sit back in your house with central heat and air-conditioning, flick on a lightbulb without fear of fire or electrocution, perhaps sip a cool beverage untainted by toxic chemicals or human waste, and let's journey back into the real "good old days." I promise, these terrifying truths about yesteryear will leave you breathing a sigh of relief that you live in the twenty-first century.

1

PATENTS
THAT SHOULD STILL
BE PENDING

Failed and foolish inventions,
and the rocky road to progress

1 ➤ For your eyes only

Shy about how you look in a swimsuit? Maybe you need a "bathing machine," invented by a Quaker in 1753. It consisted of a horse drawn half-carriage containing a "**modesty tunnel**" that allowed swimmers (fully clothed, mind you) to wade into the ocean in complete privacy.

2 ➤ They knew it like the backs of their hands

Before the invention of the blackboard in 1809 (or 1801 or 1823, depending on the account), teachers had no way to present information to all students at once. The dilemma was epitomized by Olive M. Isbell, who opened the first school in California in 1846—after the blackboard's invention, but before its arrival in the Golden State. Lacking not only a blackboard but also slates or paper, she resorted to **writing the alphabet on the backs of pupils' hands.**

3 ➤ If he'd died, we might have been spared *Xanadu*

John Joseph Merlin, the inventor of roller skates, discovered his creation's limitations the hard way in his spectacular debut at a London masquerade party in 1760: Making a grand entrance, he rolled into the ballroom atop two pairs of iron wheels, playing a violin. But, according to a contemporary account, **Merlin's skates lacked "the means of retarding his velocity or commanding its direction."** So "he impelled himself against a mirror of more than five hundred pounds value, dashed it to atoms, broke his instrument to pieces, and wounded himself most severely."

4 ➤ It's still faster than post

The laying of the first trans-Atlantic communications cable in 1858 was hailed by President Buchanan, in a cable to Queen Victoria, as "a triumph more glorious, because far more useful to mankind, than was ever won by conqueror on the field of battle." It wasn't exactly a speedy triumph, however: **The first trans-Atlantic telegram took more than seventeen hours to transmit.**

5 ➤ Short-circuit at 20,000 leagues under the sea

The "glorious" triumph of the trans-Atlantic cable would last only one month. Beneath the waves, the cable's insulation began to deteriorate. An excess of voltage, applied in hopes of speeding transmission **fried the already-vulnerable wires.** Transatlantic telegraphy would not be permanently restored for eight years.

6 ➤ If only he hadn't been so meticulous

Johann Philipp Reis, a German schoolteacher, actually beat Alexander Graham Bell in inventing the telephone by fifteen years. But Reis's invention **worked only when the electrical contacts were dusty**—and Reis ordinarily kept his equipment spotless. He died thinking his telephone was a failure.

7 ➤ Telegraphing the punch

A Western Union internal memo in 1876 dismissed the telephone as having "too many shortcomings to be seriously considered as a means of communication."

➤ These are the bounciest bullets I've ever seen!

The multitalented Alexander Graham Bell also came up with a metal detector, part of the exhaustive, if mostly wrongheaded efforts, to save the life of President James Garfield, wounded by an assassin. Bell's detector, designed to locate the bullets still within the dying president's body, worked like a charm in the lab but mysteriously failed in Garfield's sickroom. Only when it was much too late was it discovered that Bell's invention had been **detecting the metal springs in Garfield's bed instead of the assassin's bullets.**

9 ➤ Wind the alarm!

An 1870s **burglar alarm design relied on a clockwork mechanism**. You wound it up, then set a triggering lever and placed the wedge-shaped booby trap at the foot of a door, securing it with a spike pushed into the floor. An unwitting burglar opening the door would depress the lever and set off a loud alarm bell.

10 ➤ For whom the bell tolls

Responding to Victorians' fixation with the fear of being buried alive, inventor George Bateson marketed the Bateson Revival Device, advertised as "a most economical, ingenious, and trustworthy mechanism, superior to any other method, and promoting peace of mind amongst the bereaved in all stations of life. A device of proven efficacy, in countless instances in this country and abroad." Popularly known as a "Bateson's Belfry," the device, patented in 1852, used **an iron bell attached to a cord placed in the hand of the (maybe) deceased**; the least bit of subterranean motion, it was said, would ring the bell. Though the invention made Bateson wealthy, his own obsession with premature burial led him to take the drastic step of dousing himself with linseed oil and committing suicide by setting himself on fire in 1886.

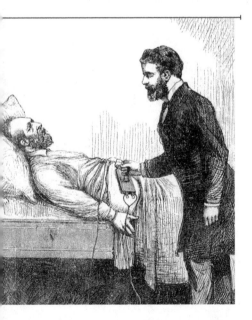

11 ➤ It's right under your nose!

Moustaches were a constant dinner time challenge for men in the nineteenth century. Among the many inventions designed to keep facial hair out of your soup (and vice versa) was a **moustache shield** patented in 1876 by Virgil A. Gates. The moustache-sized band was held in place by straps around the ears.

12 ➤ The truth comes to light

The great Thomas Edison's first major demonstration of incandescent electric lights at his Menlo Park laboratory in 1879, in which two buildings glowed with lights, was **mostly a fake**. His overworked glass blowers had been able to make only thirty-four light bulbs, so the balance was made up by old-fashioned gas lamps.

13 ➤ Whoa, Nellie!

A subsequent, grander Edison demonstration, set to debut in September 1882, involved lighting an entire section of lower Manhattan. Horses behaved skittishly around the district that was being wired for electricity—a mystery that was solved when it was found that **leaking electricity was zapping their metal horseshoes**.

14 ➤ Nothing to smile about

Edison's great Wall Street demonstration also ran into problems back at the lab. **Several of his assistants' teeth fell out because of mercury poisoning** from overexposure to the mercury pump used in making light bulbs.

15 ➤ Don't touch that wire!

But it wasn't just the "Wizard of Menlo Park" and his crew that occasionally ran afoul of the eccentricities of electricity. In 1896, Edison's former partner, Franklin Pope, **electrocuted himself while fiddling with the wiring of his own house.** The news convinced many that this newfangled electricity would never prove safe.

16 ➤ Think of it as a private fireworks display

Even after electrical sockets became common on the walls of houses—at first they were installed only overhead, as part of light fixtures—it required some courage to use them. Wall sockets commonly emitted smoke and ominous crackling sounds, and **sometimes even shot sparks out into the room.**

17 ➤ Some dense ideas

Not everything Thomas Edison touched proved so, well, electric—he had 1,093 patents, after all. Among his more half-baked ideas was an obsession with making things from cement—not just buildings, but **cement pianos and phonograph cabinets.** Although he formed the Edison Portland Cement Company to pursue his dream of cement products, it never lived up to his hopes.

18 ➤ Turning their weapons against them

Thomas Edison also developed plans to construct gigantic electromagnets for the battlefield, so powerful that not only could the magnets stop bullets in-flight, but would **send them whizzing back to shoot the enemy that had fired them.**

19 ➤ You're getting sleepy

Edison also envisioned "electrically charged atomizers" that would be able to **put enemy armies into mass comas.**

20 ➤ Write this way

The first ballpoint pen was patented in 1888 by Massachusetts tanner John Loud. His complex pen used four tiny balls, ink made from lampblack and caster oil, and **had to be held straight up and down to write**. Designed to mark on leather and other rough surfaces, Loud's pioneering pen, not surprisingly, never found true commercial application.

21 ➤ Life before programmable appliances

Tea lovers had to go to pretty convoluted lengths in the early 1900s to wake up to a piping-hot cup of their favorite beverage. One elaborate solution was to attach an alarm clock to a teakettle. **When the alarm went off, it struck a match against moving sandpaper, which lit a small burner underneath the kettle of water**. When the water boiled, the pressure of the steam would lift a hinged flap, tilting the kettle to fill a teapot waiting underneath.

22 ➤ Apparently chicken blindness was a real problem

Eyeglasses for chickens? The spectacles patented in 1902 by Andrew Jackson Jr. (no relation to the seventh president) were **designed to protect hens' eyes from being pecked by rival birds**—not (we're pretty sure) to improve their view of the barnyard.

23 ⤙ That had to suck

Early vacuum cleaners were not exactly convenient. Patented in 1901, Hubert Cecil Booth's "Puffing Billy" was so big that **it required a horse-drawn cart to reach a customer's home**. With the oil-fueled engine parked outside, a cleaning crew hauled hoses into the house through doors and windows. Nonetheless, wealthy society ladies threw "vacuum cleaner parties," where guests sipped tea and lifted their feet for Booth's uniformed crew.

24 ⤙ Vacuum and home gym all in one

Sometimes mechanized cleaning also involved a workout: The Kotten vacuum cleaner, produced in 1910, required the operator to **stand on a platform and "rock from side to side like a teeter-totter," working twin bellows**.

25 ⤙ Quite a stretch

So challenging were the musical compositions of Stravinsky, Debussy, and other composers of the age that pianists were encouraged to stretch their fingers—using **a special finger-stretching device invented in 1910**. Careful, though: It was said that Igor Stravinsky damaged his hands by employing the gizmo too vigorously.

26 ⤙ A leap of faith

The newfangled era of air travel soon brought its own ancillary inventions, not all of them as successful as the Wright Brothers'. Take, for example, the ill-fated **parachute jacket** invented by Franz Reichert in 1912. The idea was simple: Why bother with a separate parachute when you could incorporate one into your jacket? Reichert planned a headline-grabbing demonstration of the parachute jacket in which he would leap off the Eiffel Tower. He leaped. The parachute failed to deploy. He died.

27 ➤ What am I, a mind-reader?

A 1919 article envisioned **machines in every office that would read executives' minds, doing away with the need for dictation**; stenographers, however, would still be required to transcribe the CEOs' thoughts.

28 ➤ You won't want to hit "snooze"

In 1919, J.D. Humphrey patented a design for an "alarm clock" that **woke you up with a blow to the forehead**. The clock mechanism triggered a bedside baton on a pivot to drop, bonking the sleeper on the head.

29 ➤ Tomorrow's forecast is coming up ... in six months

The first attempts to use mathematical calculations to predict the weather weren't much help with whether to take an umbrella today. An early attempt at "numerical weather prediction" by mathematician Lewis Fry Richardson took **several months to calculate a six-hour forecast near Munich**—which proved wildly inaccurate. Undaunted, in a 1922 book Richardson envisioned 64,000 mathematicians performing the necessary calculations simultaneously.

30 ➤ Why do it yourself?

Henry Ford imagined a future in which everything would be done by machines, where a man would "press a button by the side of the bed and find himself **automatically clad, fed, exercised, amused, and put to bed again**."

31 ➤ You are here

A 1920s version of today's GPS navigation devices, lacking modern computers and satellites, relied instead on paper maps: **The wristwatch-sized gizmo used a series of tiny maps that owners could scroll through** using little knobs at top and bottom.

32 ➤ A lesson in stick-to-it-iveness

Masking tape, invented by Richard Drew in 1925, launched a whole industry for the Minnesota Mining and Manufacturing Co. (3M)—but it almost didn't happen. At the time, the company was focused on sandpaper. Drew visited an auto body shop in St. Paul, Minnesota, to test a new batch of sandpaper, and observed the tribulations of a crew painting the then-popular two-tone cars. Drew went back to his lab and experimented with backings and adhesives for masking tape, until company President William McKnight told him to quit fooling around and get back to sandpaper. Undeterred, Drew kept at it, **financing the tape project by writing a series of $99 purchase orders**—since he was authorized to make purchases under $100.

33 ➤ Putting the "Scotch" in tape

The first tape made by 3M was a failure, however, because it used adhesive only along the edges, which caused it to fall off. One annoyed customer told inventor Richard Drew to "take this tape back to those Scotch bosses of yours and tell them to **put more adhesive on it**"—and thus Scotch Tape was born.

34 ➤ Call for Charlie McCarthy

Ventriloquists would love the **Laryngaphone**, introduced in 1929 to help in noisy situations where background noise might compete with the caller's voice: The microphone part of the telephone handset was pressed against the throat instead of held at the mouth, so speech vibrations from the larynx were transferred directly rather than through the air.

35 ➤ Hurts so good

The "Electro Massager" of the 1930s attempted to cash in on the era's fad for body massage as a stimulant to health and good skin. The "Electro Massager" tried to go the competition one better, however, by **applying small electrical shocks as it massaged.**

36 ➤ We're glad no thumbs are involved

Not just the body was thought to benefit from a hearty massage. Hence the **Eye Massager**, invented in the 1920s. You pressed the binoculars-like device against your face and operated small rubber bellows, which puffed air into your eyes to "massage" your eyeballs.

37 ➤ Couldn't you just take a walk in the park?

The 1937 Baby Cage sought to revolutionize early child care by **suspending an infant in a wire cage that could be hung outside a window, dangling over an alley or busy street.** The idea was that city-dwelling families lacking a garden or other outdoor space could give their baby a breath of fresh air—at least until the 1930s version of Child Protective Services showed up.

38 ➤ Does it come with a matching umbrella hat?

Smoking seems to have been the inspiration for a number of questionable inventions. In 1954, for instance, Robert L. Stern of Zeus Corporation designed the Rainy Day Cigarette Holder. In case of rain, **a tiny umbrella popped up to shield the cigarette from the elements**. The smoker might get wet, but not his smoke!

39 ➤ Can't Bogart this smoke!

No need to pass a smoke back and forth with the handy "Double Ender" pipe, introduced in the late 1940s, which sported **two stems attached to a single bowl**. The manufacturer targeted pipe smokers down on their luck, who could thus split a pipeful of tobacco, and baseball fans who might want to share a smoke at a ball game.

40 ➤ One just isn't enough?

Just the opposite was the intent of a double-cigarette holder, supposedly inspired by one in the detective novels starring Bulldog Drummond: **The Y-shaped device let you smoke two cigarettes at once.** The fictional Drummond liked to smoke a Turkish cigarette and a Virginia one simultaneously.

41 ➤ Smoke 'em if you got 'em

Then there was the Cigarette Pack Holder, rolled out in 1955, which outdid the double-holder by a long stretch: **It held an entire pack of cigarettes in two V-shaped rows.** Presumably, the idea was to chain-smoke them one after another, rather than all at once.

42 ➤ Putting the Marlboro man out work

In 1909, Daniel Brown invented a cigarette-smoking automaton. The **chain-smoking robot** was designed as a promotional gimmick, appearing to smoke as it moved its arm; the actual smoke was "exhaled" from a canister beneath the automaton's chair.

43 ➤ No more ring around the collar

In the late 1940s, the Los Angeles Brush Manufacturing Corporation invented a "dry cleaner" for youngsters' necks. The plastic collar brush was supposed **to clean a child's neck without the use of soap and water while the child played**. The idea, the company said, came from a mother.

44 ➤ I'll snap the tar outta ya!

Another late-1940s Los Angeles Brush Manufacturing Corporation innovation was **the rubber-band spanking brush**. Instead of walloping a misbehaving child with a regular bristled brush, this invention replaced bristles with rubber bands, to let softhearted dads give Junior a softer spanking. This idea the company credited to a Montana father who hated using an ordinary hairbrush for discipline.

45 ➤ You're going to need a bigger desk

The first digital computer, ENIAC, completed in 1945, **weighed thirty tons and stood two stories tall**. Programming it required setting 3,000 switches and wiring cable connections, all by hand. ENIAC used 19,000 vacuum tubes, which rapidly burned out.

46 ➤ Out of sight, out of mind

If Venetian blinds work on windows, why not sunglasses? That was the idea behind **Venetian Blind Sunglasses**, introduced in 1950. One problem: When the teensy "blinds" attached to the glasses were closed, the wearer couldn't see out at all.

47 ➤ Not a straight shooter

No waiting until you see the whites of their eyes with **the curved-barrel machine gun**, introduced in 1953—in fact, you couldn't see your target at all. But that wouldn't stop you from blasting away around a corner with this M3 submachine gun whose barrel took a bend just before its business end. No need for special mind training like in *The Matrix* movie—just pull the trigger and hope!

48 ➤ You'll never want to stop mowing

Why the **Power Mower of the Future**, introduced in 1957, never caught on is a mystery. The rider sat on a foam seat atop a five-foot-diameter plastic sphere, from which you could not only mow the lawn but fertilize it, spray for bugs, and even plow snow. The mower had its own electric generating system, which also powered lights, a radio telephone, air-conditioning, and a water cooler for a refreshing drink.

49 ➤ For your listening pleasure

Before the automobile tape deck and the CD player, there was **the automobile record player**. The 1959 "Auto Minion" could be attached to your car's dashboard and played automatically when you inserted a 45 rpm record. The eight-track tape, which could hold the entire contents of an LP, proved more popular upon its introduction in the mid-1960s.

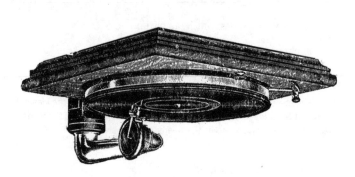

50 ➤ You'll flip for this

The 1960 New York High Fidelity Show displayed a stereo turntable that could play records even when operated upside down. The upside-down turntable never really took off, however, perhaps because of **the difficulty of reaching it on the ceiling**.

51 ➤ The magical, mystery inventor

Among the more recent failed inventors of note was Alex Mardas, better known as "Magic Alex," the name given him by the Beatles in the mid-1960s. In the days of the eight-track tape player, Mardas bragged that he could build a 72-track player, so the Fab Four set him up in the Apple Studio. In addition to the 72-track tape machine, Magic Alex also failed to deliver on his promises to make **wallpaper loudspeakers, a "sonic force field," a flying saucer, and electric paint**.

2 ARE YOU REALLY GOING TO EAT THAT?

Food, not-so-glorious food

52 ➤ Kentucky fried eagle, anyone?

Among the "delicacies" consumed in olden days besides more familiar poultry, such as chickens, ducks and geese, were **swans, herons, peacocks, and even eagles**. No bird was too small to wind up on the dinner table, including larks, finches, and sparrows.

53 ➤ No wonder they invented fish sticks

Giving up meat on Fridays or during Lent is nothing compared to the explosion of "lean" days on the calendar when the Catholic church was at its peak of influence. At one point, eating anything meatier than fish was **forbidden on nearly half the days of the year**.

54 ➤ Don't leave home without them

Silverware wasn't something our ancestors took for granted. In medieval times, knives and spoons both were part of a traveler's kit; hosts were not expected to provide either for dinner guests. Common people still ate with their hands, using **four-day-old pieces of bread called "trenchers" to push their food**.

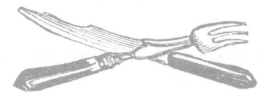

55 ➤ Dinner time dueling

Forks became popular in part because of the problem of **knife fights at dinner time**. In 1699, French King Louis XIV banned pointed knives at meals. Since blunted knives were useless for spearing food in the old two-knife dining style, forks replaced the knife held in the left hand.

56 ➤ A fork in the road of mealtime history

Americans departed from the "Continental" style of dining, in which the knife and fork are grasped in separate hands rather than switching back and forth, because of the newfangled blunt knives. When the change reached the American colonies in the early 1700s, few forks were available on this side of the Atlantic. Americans were forced to **use spoons, upside-down, to steady food for cutting**. They would then switch the spoon to the right hand, flipping it to use as a scoop. Even after forks became everyday utensils, this "zigzag" style persisted.

57 ➤ Think of it as extra texture

Before the advent of pure-food laws and food inspectors, greedy producers adulterated their products with anything they could get their hands on that was remotely similar to the real thing. (Being edible was not a requirement.) Makers of sugar and flour padded out their products with "daft," as such fillers were called, including **dirt, sand, plaster of Paris, and gypsum**.

58 ➤ Earl Grey or Earl of Sandbox?

Tea was commonly adulterated, too. One Victorian-era shipment of tea, when inspected by a suspicious buyer, turned out to be almost **half dirt and sand**.

59 ➤ Not exactly the best part of waking up

Coffee, too, was seldom entirely what it was purported to be. In the 1870s, it was common for what was sold as coffee to contain **mostly roasted peas and beans (not coffee beans), flavored with chicory**.

60 ➤ His success was clear

Food purity was important to the success of Henry J. Heinz, of "57 Varieties" fame. Heinz's very first variety, in 1869, was his mother's grated horseradish. The secret to his success? Heinz sold the horseradish in a clear glass jar to show that, unlike his competitors, **his product contained no turnip filler, leaves, or wood pulp**.

61

➤ This bread really sticks to your ribs

An anonymous book published in 1757, *Poison Detected: Or Frightful Truths*, claimed that, to save on flour, **bakers sometimes added "sacks of old bones" to their bread:** "The charnel houses of the dead are raked to add filthiness to the food of the living." Other "additives" to bread supposedly included chalk, white lead, ash, and slaked lime.

62 ➤ No wonder the cupboard was bare

Not that bread was cheap, despite such, er, cost-saving moves. In the nineteenth century, as much as **80 percent of an average family's household budget was spent on food**, and 80 percent of that expenditure went for bread.

63 ➤ Now with extra lead!

How to make those bakery products fly off the shelves? Before pesky laws intervened, **some bakers gave their goods a lovely wash of lead chromate**, said to give breads and pies a golden glow.

64 ➤ You've heard of spit and polish?

Even fruit got spiffed up, if you can call it that, to look more attractive to customers. One eighteenth-century author claimed that **cherry vendors rolled the fruit around in their mouths to make it glisten before being displayed**.

65 ➤ An apple a day will send you to the doctor

Tainted fruit was blamed for a cholera epidemic in 1832. In the aftermath of the epidemic, **New York City banned the sale of fruit**. Although the ban was rescinded a few years later, many New Yorkers remained suspicious of all fruits.

66 ➤ A latté with a shot of snot

In *The Expedition of Humphry Clinker*, a picaresque novel by Tobias Smollett published in 1771, the author describes how milk would be carried around the city in open pails. Though meant to be satirical, there was likely some truth in Smollett's description of **"spittle, snot and tobacco-squids ... spatterings from coach-wheels ... the spewings of infants" and vermin plopping into the passing milk pails."**

67 ➤ Milk roulette

Cows that fed on white snakeroot, a perennial herb common in the Ohio River Valley that contains the poison tremetol, could pass along the toxin in their milk. **Thousands, especially children, died of the mysterious "milk sickness"** until frontier physician Anna Pierce Hobbs Bixby figured out the cause, supposedly with the help of a Shawnee medicine woman. "Milk sickness" was particularly frightening because the poison milk did not smell or taste any different from milk that was safe to drink.

68 ➤ Tipsy toddlers

"Swill milk" was a profitable sideline for distilleries, which fed their waste mash and "whiskey slops" to cows and then sold the milk. **Children were said to show signs of drunkenness when given swill milk.** The distilleries' dairy cows were often so old and sick that they had to be pulled upright by cranes in order to be milked.

69 ➤ Not the 31 flavors we were hoping for

Even when foods weren't adulterated, slipshod standards of hygiene meant pretty much anything could wind up in your meal. One sample of ice cream tested in 1881, for example, was found to contain **cotton, insects, human hair, and cat hair**—in addition to, one hopes, at least a little actual ice cream.

70 ➤ Not to mention frostbite!

This may explain why ice cream, in particular, was so prone to contamination: Owners of ice-cream shops were known to **stir their frozen concoctions by plunging their bare hands and arms into the ice cream**.

71 ➤ The cold facts

Even after the turn of the twentieth century, food-borne contamination was nearly universal. One report counted **fifty million bacteria per cubic centimeter of ice cream**. In Philadelphia, 80 percent of the samples of ice cream tested contained streptococci bacteria.

72 ➤ "Frozen Frank," thankfully, did not occur to him

Another popular frozen treat, **the Popsicle, was invented by accident by an eleven-year-old boy**. In 1905, young Frank Epperson forgot his fruit juice, with a stirrer in it, outside one unusually cold night in San Francisco. When it froze and the boy sampled the result, he realized he'd discovered something—which he dubbed the Ep-cicle. Happily, when Epperson revisited his invention years later, in 1923, both the product's standards of hygiene and name were improved, and the Popsicle was a success.

73 ➤ Stop licking on my half!

So widespread was poverty during the Depression that Frank Epperson modified his original Popsicle invention to create **the "twin" Popsicle**, which could be shared by two children.

74 ➤ Something to chew on

The first attempted use of chicle, the ingredient that makes chewing gum, well, chewy, was in tires. In 1871, Thomas Adams, secretary to Mexican ex-president General Antonio Lopez de Santa Anna of Alamo fame, got a sample from the general, then living in Staten Island. Santa Anna was familiar with chicle from his days in Mexico, where Native Americans had long harvested it from the sapodilla tree. Struck by its elasticity, **Adams tried combining chicle with rubber to make carriage tires**. That flopped, so Adams invented chewing gum instead.

75 ➤ Hey, it beats a dirt sandwich!

Other foods adapted to the hard times of the Depression years included the sandwich. Among the typical lunchbox fare for coal miners was the "water sandwich"—**stale bread soaked in water and lard**.

76 ➤ Frozen Bacon

Long before Clarence Birdseye pioneered frozen food, Sir Francis Bacon gave his life to the cause. **He died in 1626 after contracting pneumonia during an experiment stuffing a chicken with snow to test its preservative properties.** Though tragic, Bacon's death inspired a witty poem: "Against cold meats was he insured? For frozen chickens he procured—brought on the illness he endured, and never was this Bacon cured."

77 ➤ Waste not, want not

The "TV dinner" was born because Carl Swanson, owner of the food-processing firm that bore his name, had **270 tons of leftover turkey.** Rather than see the turkey go bad or throw it out, Swanson packed it in aluminum trays along with gravy, corn bread stuffing, sweet potatoes and peas, freezing the whole meal.

78 ➤ Cold comfort food

There was only one problem with early frozen TV dinners: **Few people had freezers in their homes** (much less televisions, for that matter), so when they brought the dinners home from the store, they had to cook and eat them right away.

79 ➤ Maybe he should have targeted Eskimos...

The first commercial ice shipment, by Bostonian Frederic Tudor in 1806, failed miserably—and not just because of the **90 percent melting rate**. Tudor neglected to consider how his customers—in the torrid West Indies—would store the stuff once he got it to them.

80 ➤ What rhymes with rotten?

Fresh fruit didn't fare much better in shipping. In 1859, Americans eagerly awaited a shipment of 300,000 oranges sailing as fast as the wind could take the ship from Puerto Rico to New England. Despite a record-setting pace, **two-thirds of the oranges rotted** before they could enliven Yankee tables.

81 ➤ It's a long way from the ocean

Fresh seafood, today taken for granted, was beyond exotic until the advent of refrigerated railroad cars. When the first lobster arrived in Chicago in 1842, **crowds gathered to stare at the crustacean**. History does not record who was the first Chicagoan to don a lobster bib.

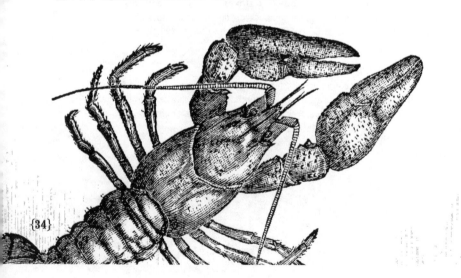

82 ➤ This butter churn seems a lot like a piñata
Butter was originally made in ancient Mesopotamia by skinning a goat, then tightly tying up the goatskin, leaving an opening at the left foreleg. Goat or sheep's milk was poured in, and **the goatskin was suspended from tent poles and swung or beaten with sticks to churn until butter formed**.

83

➤ They're always after my pot of golden butter...
In Ireland and Scotland, butter was packed in wooden "firkins" and buried in peat bogs, whose cool, anaerobic conditions enabled the butter to last indefinitely; the Irish were said to plant trees to mark butter burial sites. **The National Museum of Ireland has a firkin of bog-buried butter dating from the late seventeenth or early eighteenth century**. It now contains "a grayish cheese-like substance, partially hardened, not much like butter, and quite free from putrefaction."

84 ➤ Let's hope no one stored butter near the outhouse
Butter often picked up flavor from its storage area. Butter stored in cold seawater tasted briny, while butter kept in cellars near turnips and cabbage picked up the flavor of vegetables.

85 ➤ Waiter, there's a hoof in my butter!
"Bogus butter," sold to unsuspecting customers in the 1890s, was **a concoction of hog fat and animal parts**, bleached to resemble butter.

86 ➤ Rich, creamy ... gelatin?

Dairies adulterated their genuine butter with anything they could get their hands on, including **gypsum, gelatin, and mashed potatoes**. That was probably just as well, as the little bit of actual butter in the concoction was probably rancid, anyway.

87 ➤ The great pretender

As margarine began to threaten the dairy industry, some **states passed anti-margarine laws**, and Congress imposed the first tax on "artificial butter" with the Margarine Act of 1886. Wisconsin, the Dairy State, was the last to repeal margarine restrictions, in 1967.

88 ➤ DIY dye-job

By 1902, 80 percent of the U.S. population, in thirty-two states, lived under laws prohibiting the tinting of margarine to resemble butter. A generation of Americans grew up **coloring their own margarine with dye capsules** provided separately by the manufacturers.

89 ➤ In the pink

In an extreme effort to protect the dairy industry, **some states required margarine, naturally white, to be colored pink**.

90 ➤ A pinch of that, a bunch of this, then cook on "hot"

Early recipes were, to put it mildly, inexact. Until the breakthrough *Modern Cookery for Private Families*, published in 1845, **no cookbook bothered to include cooking times or measurements for ingredients**.

91 ➤ Tomatoes got a rotten review

Well into the nineteenth century, cooks eyed the tomato—which is, after all, a member of the deadly nightshade family—with suspicion. The dominant cookbook of the age, *Mrs. Beeton's Book of Household Management*, published in 1861, warned, "The whole plant has a disagreeable odor, and its juice, subject to the action of the fire, **emits a vapor so powerful as to cause vertigo and vomiting.**"

92 ➤ Would you like Satan's fries with that?

Although popular with the Irish, who could afford little else to eat, potatoes likewise were viewed with scorn by many—in part because their edible parts grew underground, and thus seemed unwholesome. Clergymen also pointed out that **potatoes are never mentioned in the Bible, so they must be the food of the devil.**

93 ➤ Not exactly a fair trade

The fungus that caused the Irish potato crop to fail in the 1840s, causing 1.5 million hungry Irish to emigrate to the United States, likely came from North America. So, ironically, **the trans-Atlantic shipping that would carry an unprecedented outflow of Irish to North America is probably what caused their famine in the first place.**

94 ➤ Vitamin C everywhere, but not a bite to eat

Scurvy, caused by a shortage of vitamin C in the diet, was a scourge of Forty-Niners headed to the California Gold Rush. Ironically, **the westbound fortune-seekers passed many native plants that could have cured the condition,** but didn't know to sample them.

95 ➤ Don't count your pears before they've bloomed

Even when prospectors got to California, food was scarce. Ripe pears sold for $2.50 apiece, a fortune in the mid-nineteenth century. One enterprising local was said to **sell her pears when they were still just blossoms on the tree,** tagging each flower with the name of a hungry Forty-Niner.

96 ➤ An army marches on its stomach

Confederate soldiers in the Civil War would eat the same thing every day for days on end, drawing on **meager rations of bacon, cornmeal, tea, sugar or molasses, and the occasional vegetable.** One standard meal, quickly prepared before a march, was "coosh": fried bacon, cornmeal, and water.

97 ➤ Where's the beef?

The U.S. Army's sudden demand for cheap beef to feed forces fighting the Spanish-American War led to the "Embalmed Beef Scandal," in which the three leading Chicago meat-packing companies sold the government spoiled, low-quality, adulterated beef products. The meat that reached soldiers in Cuba caused an unprecedented toll of illnesses and deaths—much of which was initially blamed on yellow fever, which causes similar symptoms. Soldiers unlucky enough to be served the beef said **it looked and tasted as though it had been slaughtered during the Civil War.**

98 ➤ That's more than a caffeine buzz

When Coca-Cola was introduced in 1886, **the recipe initially included a small amount of cocaine**. The soft-drink maker didn't take the cocaine out of Coke until 1903.

99 ➤ It has a lovely bouquet

Coca-Cola inventor Dr. John Pemberton based the famous soft drink on another, less-successful beverage he'd created—French Wine of Coca. The concoction contained **Bordeaux wine, caffeine and, of course, cocaine**.

100 ➤ Sobering statistics

In the years before Prohibition, America increasingly became a nation of drunks. **Per capita alcohol consumption rose from eight gallons in 1878 to a (literally) staggering seventeen gallons in 1898**.

101 ➤ Green, but not with envy

Among the ingredients in absinthe, all the rage in nineteenth century bohemian circles, is wormwood, which contains a potent neurotoxin. But wormwood may not be to blame for the ill effects of consuming the drink known as the "green fairy": At **60 to 75 percent alcohol**, the greenish liqueur was powerful stuff. Devotees would carry a special perforated absinthe spoon, which held a sugar cube (to counter the bitterness) over the glass of liqueur while water was added.

102 ➤ Breakfast of champion drinkers

Eggs Benedict was invented, according to one account, as a hangover cure. One morning after in 1894 at the Waldorf-Astoria, Lemuel Benedict ordered toast, bacon, poached eggs, and hollandaise sauce in hopes it would cure the previous night's excesses.

103 ➤ At least it wouldn't get soggy in milk

Breakfast cereal was invented in 1863 by Dr. James Caleb Johnson, who operated a sanitarium in Dansville, New York. The good doctor dubbed his creation "Granula," as in "granule." Not exactly a "ready-to-eat" cereal, Granula took some advance planning: **The dense bran nuggets had to be soaked overnight before serving.**

104 ➤ Apparently coffee is stronger than love

The world's first coffeehouse, Kiva Han, began catering to Turks' java joneses in Istanbul in the 1470s. Turkish coffee was brewed strong and black in a pot called an "ibrik"; **Turkish women were allowed to divorce their husbands if the men could not keep the ibrik filled.**

105 ➤ You might want to freshen up your coffee

Early coffeehouses fixed their cups o' joe in a way that would make today's java junkies shudder: **Coffee was brewed in large batches, stored cold in barrels, and reheated for serving**, thereby minimizing waste and the toll of high taxes on coffee.

106 ➤ Don't stand behind them, they might shoot!

"Texas red" chili was apparently the favorite food of bank robbers. Legendary outlaw brothers **Frank and Jesse James would stoke up for their heists by downing some chili.** Their favorite chili came from Fort Worth, where they vowed never to rob the bank, saying, "Anyplace that has a chili joint like this just oughta be treated better."

107 ➤ Sticky situation

In 1919, a burst molasses tank at the U.S. Industrial Alcohol Co. in Boston spilled 2.5 million sticky gallons through the city's streets. **An eight-foot-high wave of molasses** destroyed a firehouse, toppled elevated train lines, and killed twenty-one people.

3 RATS AND OTHER FASHION ACCESSORIES

Style and beauty back then

108 ➤ A deadlier shade of pale

Before tanning booths, pale skin was considered desirable as a sign of a life of leisure, rather than working outdoors. As far back as ancient Greece and Rome, people lightened their complexions with makeup containing chalk, animal fats, starch, and powders or pastes of white lead, which can cause **disfigurement and death**.

109 ➤ The white queen

Deadly makeup remained fashionable into the Elizabethan era, when women applied ceruse—**a compound of white lead and vinegar**—in imitation of the queen's pallid skin.

110 ➤ Max Factor, meet Count Dracula

Over the years, almost everything has been tried to achieve a fashionably pale complexion. In the sixth century, **women sometimes bled themselves to look more pale**.

111 ➤ The breakfast of beauties

Other approaches to achieve a pale complexion have included **eating chalk and drinking iodine**. In the nineteenth century, whitening concoctions also incorporated mercury, silver nitrate, and acid.

112 ⤞ Darling, your skin looks ... poisoned

Introduced in 1786 as a patent medicine, Fowler's Solution became a popular tonic that women drank to improve their complexions. The complexion enhancer was actually a solution of **potassium arsenite, a compound of arsenic that could poison the user as well as cause cancer**.

113 ⤞ No, Chanel No. 5 is not an SPF number...

A "healthy" tan, rather than a deathly pale complexion, began to become popular in the 1920s after fashion icon Coco Chanel spent too much time out in the sun on a trip to the French Riviera. Instead of staying out of sight, she showed off her darker hue. Inspired by her example and subsequent swimsuit ads, women began to bathe in the sun's cancer-causing UV rays, **protected only by a sheen of baby oil**.

114 ⤞ Her eyebrows looked a little mousy

Before the invention of the eyebrow pencil, the facially fashion-conscious sometimes resorted to pasting on **artificial eyebrows made from mouse skin**.

115 ⤞ You might want to have that looked at

In the late 1700s and early 1800s, it became fashionable to attach artificial moles, called *mouches*, to the face. Although at first a single such patch sufficed, as the fashion reached its ridiculous extremes, both men and women began to sport multiple *mouches*, not only on the face but on the neck and even the shoulders. The **man-made moles also came in various shapes, from simple moons and stars to elaborate scenes** combining several *mouches*.

116 ⤳ My, what big eyes you have!

"Belladonna" translates as "beautiful lady," and women took the plant's name literally: They used belladonna eyedrops, because the toxins would **dilate the pupils, elevate the heart rate, and blur the vision** (perhaps making their dates seem more handsome). Overuse of belladonna—also known as deadly nightshade—could result in blindness.

117 ⤳ If only you could still see yourself in the mirror!

The use of toxic eye compounds continued into the twentieth century, with the U.S. Food and Drug Administration not empowered to regulate cosmetics until 1938. Part of the trigger for that regulatory expansion was the **1933 epidemic of blindness linked to an eyelash dye product called Lash Lure**. The permanent dye contained a toxic chemical, paraphenylenediamine, whose dangers didn't come to light until the case of a Lash Lure customer known in court records only as "Mrs. Brown." Within hours of applying the product to her eyebrows, Mrs. Brown began suffering stinging and burning in her eyes, which soon ulcerated and swelled shut. She and at least fifteen other women were blinded by Lash Lure.

118 ⤳ Hair today, gone tomorrow

To appear to have higher foreheads, then in fashion, ladies of the 15th century painfully **plucked the front of their hairlines**. What hair remained was then pulled tightly back, the better to show off the elaborate headdresses that were de rigueur for the upper classes.

119 ⤳ Golden locks, if you can stand the smell

To emulate the fair locks of Scandinavian women, women in the 15th century **bleached their hair with saffron or onion skins**—or exposed their hair to the sun for hours every day.

120 ➤ That might hinder your beauty sleep

The elaborate, towering coiffures of the eighteenth century took so long to create that weeks went by between stylings. Over time, the mixture of lard, starch, and powder, applied over cage frames or horsehair pads, **attracted rats and other vermin**, who found these high hairdos not only handy for nesting materials but for actual nesting. Some women wore cages over their heads while they slept to keep the critters away.

121 ➤ Cheep thrills

Elaborate eighteenth-century hairdos sometimes deliberately included living things. Some women embraced the idea of hairdo habitats and incorporated birdcages—**complete with feathered occupants**—into their coiffures.

122 ➤ Being of sound mind and great hair…

Men, too, were prone to hair-fashion foibles, and wigs became so important to gentlemen by the seventeenth century that **large wigs would be singled out in wills as a valuable part of an estate**.

123 ➤ Do you feel a sudden breeze?

As wig prices soared, **wig thieves began to prey on unwary gentlemen**. Some specialized in attacking hackney coaches, slicing an opening in the back, snatching a wig and scrambling away with their prize.

124 ➤ Bake his head!

So much flour was used for whitening wigs instead of baking bread that **some cities had wig riots**, in which hungry citizens protested the price of fashion.

125 ➤ It looks so real

The wig craze even affected the lower classes, who coiffed and powdered their actual hair to make it look like they were wearing (and could afford) a wig. At the bottom end of society, even slaves fashioned **makeshift wigs from cotton and goat hair**.

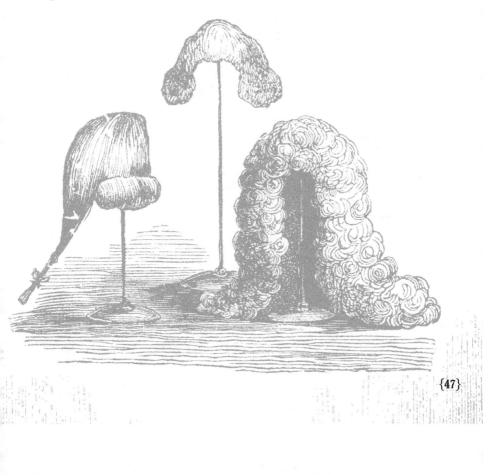

126 ➤ Still no hair, but a strange tingling sensation...

Baldness cures and hair restorers were fixtures of nineteenth-century traveling medicine shows and early mail-order catalogs. By 1893, Dr. Condit Cutler wrote of the profusion of baldness cures, "The remedies which are recommended and advertised for the cure of this affliction are exceeded in number only by those given for the relief of vomiting in pregnancy." The ingredients of these elixirs, however, resembled a cross between an exotic entrée and paint thinner: Baldness cures contained **borax, olive oil, sulphur, lead acetate, bone marrow, and extracts from the blister beetle** (better known today as the "Spanish fly").

127 ➤ Business is booming, boss!

Hollywood mogul Darryl Zanuck got his start writing ads for Yuccatone Hair Restorer, made from the yucca plant used by Native Americans. His slogan, "You've Never Seen a Bald-Headed Indian," helped made the Yuccatone a success. But the Yuccatone saga came to an abrupt end when **bottles of the hair restorer fermented and exploded in twenty-five drugstores**. The company went out of business, while Zanuck went on to work with Mack Sennett and Charlie Chaplin.

128 ➤ Getting a head start

Taking a "physician, heal thyself" approach to hair loss, in 1908 John Breck, a Massachusetts paper chemist, set out to develop a cure for his own baldness and concocted a variety of potions. The "Breck" name today adorns a line of popular shampoos and other hair-care products, and Breck died a millionaire in 1965. **But he was still bald.**

129

➤ It's all in your head

But why buy a bottle of hair tonic when you can simply think your way to a full head of hair? In the early twentieth century, French psychologist Émile Coué de la Châtaignerai—who coined the phrase, "Every day, in every way, I'm getting better and better"—applied his positive-thinking technique to baldness. Repeating his "better and better" phrase, Coué claimed, could cause hair follicles to regain lost elasticity and begin regrowing. **Bald men who were "too lazy to say the words" could record them on a phonograph and simply listen until their hair sprouted**. Modestly, Coué protested, "I do not work miracles. I am neither a god nor a saint. I am only a man."

130 ➤ A cure for hat hair

Men who still had their hair could automatically comb it with **the Comb Cap** patented in 1920. The "combined head covering and hair comb" was a flat cap that concealed a comb, so whenever a man took off his cap, the comb would run through his hair.

131 ➤ Raindrops keep falling on my ... back
There were many attempts to combine protection from the elements with head-gear, such as Joseph Smith's 1898 patent for an umbrella hat. The umbrella-shaped headgear extended several inches beyond the wearer's ears—**sluicing rain onto the back and shoulders**.

132 ➤ They hit odor with their purses
Purses developed in part as a portable response to the lack of personal hygiene. Aristocrats would carry "swete bags," filled with sweet-smelling herbs or perfumed balls of cotton, **designed to counteract the less-sweet smell of humanity**.

133 ➤ Weddings and a funeral
Brides of modest means in the nineteenth century often owned only one dress—so that's what they got married in. Women were thus frequently married wearing **wedding dresses of black or other dark colors—which could also double as funeral attire**.

➤ Women of steel
Corsets had to be made as tough as a knight's armor, although with the goal being to keep a woman's body in rather than to keep arrows and swords out. In the fifteenth century, Eleonora di Toledo, wife of Cosimo I de Medici, owned several **steel corsets that were fashioned by Cosimo's armorer**.

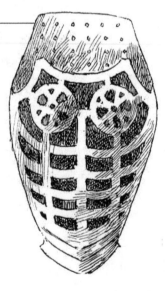

135 ➤ Squished for beauty

Corsets were worn so tight that women found it hard to breathe, and **the constricting garments were blamed for miscarriages**. Such concerns led the Republic of Venice to pass a law banning corsets in 1547.

136 ➤ Trapped!

Until the introduction of the steel-front busk fastener in 1829, **women could not put on or take off their corsets by themselves**.

137 ➤ Take it all off!

Even so, removing a corset—with its yards of fabric, bustles, and whalebone hoops—remained quite an undertaking, **whose elaborateness inspired the strip tease**.

138 ➤ If only my liver were thinner

By the late nineteenth century, **the "ideal" woman's waistline was a corset-assisted eighteen inches**, leaving precious little room for such necessities as internal organs.

139 ➤ Two to tango, one to remove the corset

One reason for the decline in popularity of the corset was **the tango craze in 1915**. Just try doing the tango in a corset!

140 ➤ Talk about a hot outfit

Even as women artificially shrank their waistlines, they began to wear "panniers" that exaggerated their hips to outrageous—and even dangerous—extremes. In the late eighteenth century, women whose panniers came in contact with an open flame sometimes **caught their gowns on fire**.

141 ➤ Swan song

A fashionable but injudicious choice of fabric could also lead to an inferno. **Women who wore wide sleeves and crinolines of tulle or gauze were walking torches** in the era of candles and other open flames. Emma Livry, a prima ballerina in the 1850s, died when her petticoat-puffed tutu was ignited by a gas lamp.

142 ➤ Hello, petticoat junction!

By the 1850s, well-dressed women adopted the crinoline, a stiffened petticoat or rigid skirt-shaped structure of steel designed to mold the skirts of a woman's dress into the required shape. This looked lovely unless the woman took a spill: If a woman fell, the crinoline would splay all about her like a three-dimensional fan, **exposing whatever was beneath**.

143 ➤ Stuck in the upright position

In the Victorian era, women had to put their shoes on midway through getting dressed, rather than waiting until their outfits were complete. The reason? Once their layers of skirts and petticoats were all in place, **women couldn't bend over**.

144

➤ Be careful stepping out in this skirt

Tighter skirts replaced billowing outfits around the turn of the twentieth century, with the trend reaching its ultimate extreme in the "**hobble skirt**." The extremely skinny skirts forced their wearers to take tiny, mincing, "geisha-like" steps. Critics denounced the hobble skirt as unsafe, and some employers banned them. Some saw an upside to the fashion, however: "Grandmothers think that the means justify the end, and that the hobble skirt will bring back to women the old grace. They will be compelled to shorten their strides, learn to place their feet in a straight line, and not throw them in or out in the slovenly modern way, and that the entire appearance of women will be thus benefited."

145 ➤ Breaking her stride

To keep women from ripping their hobble skirts, fashion mavens followed with the "**hobble garter**," which restricted the wearer's stride. A 1910 catalog described it: "This new dress adjunct may be best described as consisting of two silken garters fastened below the knees with bejewelled clasps (they are not cheap articles) and ornamented with bows of the same shade as the elastic and ribbon used. These are in turn connected by the use of a strap of elastic webbing of the same color, not over a foot in length. It can be readily seen that so equipped the danger of tripping, missteps, or of damaging the gown is minimized, and all this in detriment to the natural gait which is entirely lost by its use."

146 ➤ Now you know Victoria's secret

The original bra was nothing more than **a pair of handkerchiefs tied together with ribbons**. Mary Phelps Jacob came up with it in 1913 and later sold the patent, such as it was, to Warner Brothers. Cup sizes didn't come along until 1935, and initially came in just four options—A, B, C, and D.

147 ➤ Head and shoulders above the rest

The ultimate in the history of high-heeled shoes may have been the chopine, **a slipper mounted on a platform that in later fashions reached thirty inches high**. Wealthy women would go out with servants supporting them on either side. The chopine was particularly popular with prostitutes, however, because it raised them to heights where they could more easily be seen by potential customers.

148 ➤ Running the "race" in heels

Victorians brought back the high heel in part for racial reasons. The feet of white Europeans, they reasoned, had a high instep arch—emphasized by high heels—while Africans were thought to have little or no instep.

149 ➤ Must have been written by men

Marketers of high heels claimed that the shoes improved a woman's health by **reducing the stress of walking and alleviating backaches**.

150 ➤ Not to mention damage to bureaucrats

Introduced in the 1950s, **"stiletto" heels were often so sharply tipped that they were banned from public buildings** because of risked physical damage to the floors.

151 ➤ Back to the drawing board ... again

Originally designed to replace the fastening on high-button shoes, **the zipper was initially too complex** and would-be inventor Whitcomb L. Judson frustrated his financial backers for twenty years. Ultimately, another inventor at the same floundering company, Otto Frederick Gideon Sundback, solved the problem.

152 ➤ Talk about a "reboot"

The word **"zipper" was coined by B.F. Goodrich for zip-up rubber galoshes**. "Zipper Boot" replaced the less-zippy "Mystik Boot."

153 ➤ Don't lose your girdle over it

Though DuPont had developed nylon in the 1930s, nylon stockings weren't widely available until May 15, 1940, designated as "N-day." Desperate women (or their beleaguered husbands, instructed not to return home without the prize) thronged stores in a "battle of nylons." One newspaper headlined the havoc, "Girl Collapses, Woman Loses Girdle at Nylon Sale." **Some 780,000 pairs of stockings were sold in a single day**.

154 ➤ Those are some sheer stockings

Women who couldn't get their hands on nylons or silk stockings, which became scarce with the outbreak of World War II, made do by **drawing a line up the backs of their legs with eyeliner to simulate the look of wearing hosiery.**

155 ➤ You'd look better in khaki, pal

War, not changing tastes, caused **the demise of the Zoot Suit**. The popular and flashy men's outfit ran up against fabric restrictions from the War Production Department, which dictated that fabric should be conserved for soldiers fighting World War II.

156 ➤ Why not just wear a wet blanket?

In the late 1800s, the first women's garments designed for "bathing" (not called "swimming suits" until 1921) sported **wool or flannel padded bloomers and black wool stockings, over which was worn a knee-length dress**. Ruffled hats and shoes finished off the outfit.

157 ➤ You're showing too much elbow

Modesty ruled swimwear well into the twentieth century. In 1907, Australian swimmer Annette Kellerman was **charged with indecent exposure** when she appeared in Boston clad in a one-piece suit that scandalously bared her arms and legs.

158 ➤ Call it a swimming kilt

Men were also expected to cover up when hitting the beach. In "Bathing Suit Regulations" published in 1917, the American Association of Park Superintendents **required men to wear a "skirt" outside their swimming trunks**. Flannel knee pants and a vest front were optional attire.

159 ➤ Dare to bare

One way men sought to circumvent swimsuit prudery was the "Topper," introduced in 1932, which sported a detachable shirt that could be zipped free of the trunks to bare a man's chest. **Early adopters, however, often unzipped only to get arrested for indecent exposure.**

160 ➤ Kelp is the new black

The quest for new materials from which to fashion swimwear sometimes took ridiculous turns. In 1923, Pearl Howell, a New York ballet dancer, showed off **a bathing suit crafted entirely from seaweed**.

161 ➤ Now you see it...

Then there was the "cloque" fabric tried by Seamless Rubber Company in 1936. Swimsuits made from the crinkly rubber not only were hot and clammy but **tended to peel off in the surf**. The company later found success with "cloque" as a material for bathing caps.

162 ➤ Boil, toil, and trouble

Taking care of one's clothing in yesteryear could be an ordeal (at least for servants). Until the early twentieth century, for instance, shoe and boot polish was not widely available as a commercial product. To keep footwear shiny, as fashion demanded, required **boiling up a pot of polish at home—which stained anything it touched**.

163 ➤ Try it for shirts as crisp as potato chips

Need to starch a shirt? Forget today's convenient spray-can starch: Originally, **starch for laundry use had to be extracted from potatoes**.

164 ➤ Stain, what stain?

Similarly, before modern commercial laundry bleach, **clothes were sometimes soaked in old urine to bleach out stains**. Of course, then you had a whole 'nother problem to deal with, requiring still further laundering.

165 ➤ Keeping up appearances is never cheap

In the early twentieth century, when a schoolteacher might earn only $500 a year, one expert calculated that **it would cost $150 a year to maintain "an immaculate appearance."**

166 ➤ That's a groovy jacket, man

That unfortunate fashion fad of the 1960s, the Nehru jacket, really did originate in India, in the 1940s, where it was called a Band Gale Ka coat ("closed-neck coat"). More practical than the traditional knee-length Achkan or sherwani coats, the jacket allowed Indian men to dress formally without adopting the Western suit-coat. Made famous by musicians including the Beatles and the Monkees, the Nehru jacket was embraced perhaps most enthusiastically by **Sammy Davis Jr., who boasted that he owned two hundred Nehru jackets**.

167 ➤ Heeeere's ... an attempted fashion revival

Johnny Carson was paid to wear Nehru jackets on his *Tonight Show* in the mid-1970s in a doomed attempt to bring the jackets back into fashion.

4 HANG 'EM HIGH OR DRAWN AND QUARTERED?

Crime and punishment through the ages

168 ➤ Martyrdom by wild kingdom

About 209 AD, a group of Christian martyrs that included future saints Perpetua and Felicitas and their catechist, Saturus, were **executed by being set upon by a succession of animals**. Saturus was first lashed to a boar, which turned on its handler instead, then attacked by a bear, and ultimately killed by a leopard. A wild cow was unleashed on the women, who were then finished off by the sword. Perpetua's Roman executioner was a novice, however, and made the process so slow that she finally "herself set the sword upon her own neck."

169 ➤ Going to pieces

Though "death by a thousand cuts" is a mathematical exaggeration, public butchering was an accepted method of execution, called lingchi, in China until 1905. The Chinese had a special horror of dismemberment, fearing they would likewise be mutilated in the afterlife. So, to impress upon the public the consequences of misbehavior, authorities **hauled the condemned into a marketplace and sliced him up**: breasts cut off, next chunks of flesh from thighs and arms, then limbs removed, and finally the head.

170 ➤ Hope you've learned your lesson!

The official punishment for treason in England from 1283 to 1867 was drawing and quartering. "Drawing" apparently referred to dragging the prisoner to the place of execution, either behind a horse or on a sledge. The traitor was then hanged, but not to the point of actually dying. No, more was to come: Cut down, the semi-hanged prisoner got to **watch himself being disemboweled and see his own entrails burned**. Finally, he was beheaded and then "quartered"—his body cut or ripped by horses into four parts, one limb to a quarter.

171 ➤ Anyone for a swim?

First used by the Dutch in 1560 and not officially abolished until 1856, "keelhauling" was a punishment for sailors that involved tying the offender to a rope looped underneath the ship. **The person was then thrown overboard and dragged under water along the barnacle-encrusted keel.** Half-drowned and scraped raw, the wayward sailor was unlikely to repeat his offense.

172 ➤ No insect repellent allowed

Perhaps the most elaborate—and grotesque—technique of capital punishment was the early method known as "scaphism" (from the Greek for "hollowed out"). The condemned was stripped naked, forced to gorge on milk and honey, and covered with more honey to attract insects. He was then fastened to a pair of floating boats on a stagnant pond, where **insects would come and feed on him**—as well as breeding within his exposed flesh. One person condemned to death by scaphism was said to endure this torture for seventeen days before dying.

173 ➤ Capital ideas

Among the other creative ways that people in the past have come up with to administer the death penalty are "breaking" on a wheel, **crushing by an elephant**, boiling to death, and shooting out of a gun.

174 ➤ Eat and drink for tomorrow you die

The tradition of allowing a prisoner sentenced to death to select a last meal before his execution goes back to ancient Greece. With **no need to count calories**, for example, convicted Lindbergh-baby kidnapper Bruno Richard Hauptmann dined on celery, olives, chicken, French fries, buttered peas, cherries, and a slice of cake before his 1936 electrocution.

175 ➤ A little late to start worrying about cavities

In his pre-execution feast in 1958, Utah double-murderer Clarence Ray Allen dined on buffalo steak, fried chicken, sugar-free pecan pie, and sugar-free black walnut ice cream. It's not known why he was **concerned about his sugar intake before being hanged**.

176

➤ Finger-lickin' good until the end...

Among **the more popular last-meal requests by condemned convicts is Kentucky Fried Chicken**. In 1980, prior to being executed by lethal injection, serial killer John Wayne Gacy Jr. ordered a final dinner including a bucket of "original recipe" chicken from KFC.

177 ➤ Lobster, steak or Cheez Doodles? That's a toughie

Condemned prisoners haven't always taken full advantage of the ritual of the last meal. In 1984, Velma Barfield, sentenced to lethal injection for a half-dozen murders in North Carolina, ordered only **a bag of Cheez Doodles** and a twelve-ounce can of Coca-Cola.

178 ➤ Just Jack

From 1888 to 1891, eleven women were gruesomely killed in London's "Whitechapel murders"—at least five of them murdered by Jack the Ripper. The gory fate of the first victim, prostitute Mary Ann Nichols, set the pattern: **Her throat was cut and her lower abdomen sliced open**. The killer (or killers) was never caught.

179

➤ A little jazz keeps the bogeyman away

Though not as famous as Jack the Ripper, the Axeman of New Orleans attacked a dozen people with his trademark axe from May 1918 to October 1919. At the peak of his spree, the Axeman supposedly sent a letter saying he would kill again at 12:15 A.M. on March 20, but **would spare the customers of any establishment where jazz was playing**. New Orleans' dance halls were packed that night and many home-owners hired bands for protection. No one got the axe that night. The Axeman was never caught.

180 ➤ Don't lose your head

Between 1935 and 1938, the Cleveland Torso Murderer, also known as the Mad Butcher of Kingsbury Run, killed and dismembered at least a dozen victims. Because most were unidentified drifters and the killer was never caught, the actual death toll may have been higher—perhaps as many as fifty from the 1920s to the 1950s, ranging as far as Pittsburgh and Youngstown. **Victims were always beheaded and often dismembered**, with male victims usually castrated.

181 ➤ He has killer style

Plainfield, Wisconsin, serial killer Ed Gein, who murdered fifteen women between 1947 and 1957, was the inspiration for Alfred Hitchcock's thriller *Psycho* and the character of Buffalo Bill in *The Silence of the Lambs*, among others. Gein's unusually gruesome modus operandi may have been what caught the attention of filmmakers and novelists: **He skinned his victims and decorated his home with parts of their bodies**, making dust bins, furniture, and even clothing out of pieces of the murdered women.

182 ➤ Striking a cord

The Boston Strangler terrorized the city from June 1962 until 1964. Albert DeSalvo, a mental patient, **bragged of killing the thirteen women** but was never convicted of the murders; he was given a life sentence for an unrelated armed robbery.

183 ➤ Missing your stop is the least of your worries

Horse-drawn streetcars were hotbeds of crime. One passenger who'd apparently learned the hard way advised, "Before boarding a car, prudent persons leave their purses and watches in the safe deposit company and **carry bowie knives and derringers.**"

184 ➤ A handgun that matches your shoes...

So common was crime in the nineteenth century that an enterprising manufacturer combined a **ladies' purse with a secret compartment that hid a small, derringer-like pistol.** The owner had to be a crack shot, however, because the pistol held only a single bullet.

185 ➤ The invention of mugging

Except for the busiest, best-lit streets, **cities in the 1870s were unsafe after dark.** Visitors to New York City were advised to get a police escort if they wanted to go to a dance hall, and Central Park was too crime-ridden to enter at night.

186 ➤ It's safer to play in traffic

Pedestrians in crime-ridden cities in the nineteenth century learned to **walk down the middle of a street rather than using sidewalks**, to lessen the risk of a sap-wielding thief assailing them from adjacent doorways or alleys.

187 ➤ Attack of the hobos

Roving bands of vagabonds—far from the stereotype of the happy-go-lucky hobo— terrorized rural communities. In the 1890s, it was estimated that **the United States had 50,000 tramps**—more than the population of most cities. Some towns were so plagued by thieving hobos that the residents gave up and abandoned their homes.

188 ➤ Far from the city's finest

Police corruption was so rampant that, in 1857, the New York legislature simply **abolished New York City's municipal police force** and attempted to replace them with a newly minted police department administered from Albany.

189 ➤ Those badges come with a price, literally

Things quickly returned to police business as usual in New York City, however. By 1894, an investigative committee reported on "the systematic and pervasive impact of bribery." Given the lucrative potential of police work, it was little wonder that the jobs themselves were for sale, according to a scale as fixed as the prices in any department store: **You could buy a patrolman's position for a mere $100, but a captain's job would cost you $1,500.**

190 ➤ Judges love black and blue

Criminals who did get caught got rough treatment beginning well before they landed in prison. An 1894 investigation of police brutality in New York City reported that **rookie cops who neglected to beat up suspects were reprimanded by their superiors**. Police were expected to "mark" those they arrested with a good thrashing, so they would "have something to show in court."

191 ➤ Uncommon decency

Baring skin, even to go swimming, was a criminal offense into the twentieth century. Many U.S. cities passed **laws requiring bathing-suit-clad women to also don stockings**. Coney Island officials in 1919 arrested a woman for wearing a bathing suit in public—under her street clothes.

192 ➤ Just another downtown shootout...

Yes, Wild West gunfighters really did shoot it out in the streets. The model for the classic gunfight was a confrontation between "Wild Bill" Hickok and Davis Tutt, who had argued over a debt, in Springfield, Missouri, in 1865. Facing off near the town square, the men approached to a distance of fifty yards, drew and fired. **Hickok shot Tutt through the heart**. Tutt missed. Hickok was tried for manslaughter but acquitted.

193 ➤ Sleeping with the fishes

Gangsters really did encase victims in "cement shoes." According to underworld lore, among the first such reported mob hits was Danny Walsh, a bootlegging king-pin from Providence, Rhode Island, who was said to have been "**stood in a tub of cement until it hardened about his feet, and then thrown alive into the sea**" in 1933.

194 ➤ A bump in the road

Sometimes the mob didn't bother with the watery part of "watery grave." In 1940, the Associated Press reported a gangland rumor that the gangland assassins of Murder, Inc., had simply **tossed mobster Harry Westone into a cement mixer**. Thoroughly coated—not just his feet—Westone was then added to the paving of a New York highway.

195 ➤ Rethink your next purchase

Debtors were sent to prison—where, adding insult to injury, they were required to pay for their keep—in the United States until about the 1830s and England as late as 1869. **As little as sixty cents' worth of debt could send a person to the slammer.**

196 ➤ Getting to know you...

Before the idea of individual cells caught on in the nineteenth century, in England, inmates of all types and ages, male and female, might be crowded together in a single cell; an **eighteen-square-foot room might hold thirty to forty people**.

197 ➤ That's the spirit!

Early jailers charged fees for everything from food and clothing to locking or unlocking cell doors and leg irons. Many **jailers also operated bars**: In Philadelphia's Walnut Street prison, the jailer sold twenty gallons of liquor daily to his charges.

198

➤ This is reform?

In the 1790s, prison reformer Jeremy Bentham proposed three stages of prisons, the most awful of which was the "Black Prison," in which **inmates would be kept company by two skeletons**, slumped together on either side of an iron door as a reminder that there was no escape.

199 ➤ Some alone time
America's first true penitentiary—Eastern State Penitentiary, constructed in Philadelphia beginning in 1822—was built as a showcase for the penal-reform theory known as the "separate system" or the Pennsylvania System. In practice, it was **little more than solitary confinement**. The reformers of the Pennsylvania Prison Society described the plan: "Each prisoner was to be provided with a cell from which they would rarely leave and each cell had to be large enough to be a workplace and have attached an individual exercise yard."

200 ➤ Who's sorry now?
Proponents of the Pennsylvania System believed in penance (hence "penitentiary"), and each concrete cell at Eastern State was constructed with a single glass skylight, dubbed the "Eye of God." Inmates who proved insufficiently penitent suffered tortures including winter dousing in freezing water, **chaining their tongues to their wrists**, and confinement in a lightless pit dug under cell block 14, dubbed "The Hole."

201 ➤ They know how to kill a conversation

The alternative to the Pennsylvania System was the Silent or Auburn System, named for New York State's Auburn Prison. Inmates slept in individual cells, as small as two-by-six-feet, but worked in communal shops during the day while adhering to a **rule of silence enforced by whipping.**

202 ➤ From jailbirds to war hawks

In 1864, as the Civil War went literally and figuratively South, Georgia hit upon a solution to prison overcrowding as well as its soldier shortage: **Any inmate who agreed to fight for the Confederacy was simply pardoned and issued a gun**, trading his convict's uniform for Confederate gray.

203 ➤ Rent-to-reform

As its prisons filled up again after the Civil War, Georgia adopted the "convict lease system," **renting out prison laborers for about ten dollars a year** to mines, turpentine factories, and ironworks.

204 ➤ Feeling caged in

After Georgia's legislature banned the convict lease system in 1897, the state turned to chain gangs. By 1929, Georgia had 140 prison camps that housed convict laborers, who were shuttled to work sites—and **sometimes spent the night—in rolling cages**. The system became infamous after a book by escapee Robert E. Burns, *I Am a Fugitive from a Georgia Chain Gang*, and a 1932 movie adaptation, *I Am a Fugitive from a Chain Gang.*

205 ➤ What will the neighbors think

Even before chain gangs gained national infamy, some locals complained. A 1912 edition of the Turner County, Georgia, *Banner* noted: "There has been some complaint to this body relative to the Warden **whipping convicts on the public roads** near the residences of some of the citizens, we would suggest that the Warden be a little more careful in this respect and not whip them near the residences of any of the citizens nor on public roads."

206 ➤ At least now they can't run away

In the early 1940s, *Life* magazine ran an exposé on the inhumane conditions of Georgia chain gangs and prisons. At one site, **inmates were said to cut their own heel tendons and break their own legs** in order to avoid the heavy labor. Governor Ellis Arnall responded with a program of prison reform—which, along with his opposition to the Ku Klux Klan, cost him re-election.

207 ➤ Check for a file in his kibble

In 1924, Pennsylvania Governor Gifford Pinchot sentenced a **"cat-murdering dog"** to Eastern State Penitentiary. The canine, Pep, "convicted" of killing a cat belonging to Pinchot's wife, was assigned inmate number C2559.

208 ➤ Another solution to prison overcrowding

Sometimes prison guards took their orders to keep inmates under lock and key too literally, with tragic results. In 1930, two troublesome prisoners set fire to a wooden roof at the dangerously overcrowded Ohio State Penitentiary in Columbus, home to 4,300 inmates. Wind spread the flames and smoke to the rest of the prison, but **the chief guard refused to unlock any cells**—even as those within screamed as the blazing ceilings rained fire and collapsed—until he got official orders to do so. By the time a rescue effort finally began, 322 trapped prisoners had perished in the fire.

209 ➤ What, no shuffleboard?

California's first prison was a ship, the 268-ton U.S.S. *Waban*, anchored in San Francisco Bay. Such **"prison hulks" were a common way of housing convicts** until penitentiaries, such as San Quentin, began to be built.

210 ➤ That really cut down on complaints about the food

Alcatraz, originally a military prison, was turned over to the Justice Department in 1934 for a federal penitentiary—the predecessor of today's "Supermax" prisons. Already ringed by the frigid water of San Francisco Bay, Alcatraz was rebuilt by Robert Burge, a leading security expert, to be escape-proof. Gun galleries overlooked the cell blocks and **tear gas canisters were installed in the cafeteria ceiling**.

211 ➤ Only the bare essentials

Alcatraz had its own "Hole," as well as an even more feared "Strip Cell" in which inmates were **confined in the dark without clothes or toilet facilities,** only a hole in the floor.

212 ➤ The sound of one hand clapping

The severe rules and rigid silence in Alcatraz drove some inmates insane. Rufe Persful, a convicted bank robber, **chopped off the fingers of one of his own hands** with a hatchet.

213 ➤ Send in the Marines!

In 1946, an escape attempt by Bernard Coy triggered "the Battle of Alcatraz," in which **U.S. Marines bombarded and stormed the island prison;** two officers and three inmates were killed.

214 ➤ In this corner, wearing black-and-white-striped trunks...

All was not entirely grim at Alcatraz. When it was still an Army prison, in the late 1920s, inmates built a ball field and got to wear baseball uniforms for games. Sports fans from the mainland would arrive to watch **regularly scheduled Friday-night "Alcatraz fights"** between inmates.

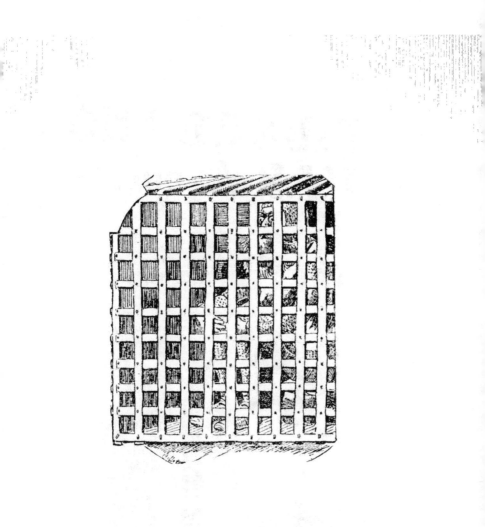

5 FIRST, DO NO HARM—OOPS!

Medicine's painful past

215 ➤ The first cut is the deepest
In the seventeenth century, **surgeons were more akin to barbers than to physicians** (who were considered gentlemen). Surgeons received no formal training, only an apprenticeship, and were principally skilled at wielding sharp blades.

216 ➤ In and out in sixty seconds or less
A common early surgical operation was "cutting of the stone," as in kidney stones—performed without benefit of anesthesia or modern notions about sterilizing instruments. The surgeon would make a three-inch incision, after which he would have **less than a minute to find and remove the stone before the patient began to bleed to death**.

217 ➤ Can I get a 9 A.M. appointment?
A little-appreciated secret to surviving surgery before modern sterilization techniques was to be the first patient of the day. The reason was simple: The surgeon's hands and instruments, ordinarily **cleaned only after a hard day of cutting people up**, would still be (relatively) clean.

218 ➤ You won't feel a thing...
Almost as awful as the lack of anesthesia were the ways physicians attempted to counter or prevent a patient's pain during treatment. One method was to **bleed the patient until the person almost passed out**, then commence with surgery during which still more blood would be spilled.

219 ➤ Think of it as snuff
Some physicians thought they could dull the agony of surgery sans anesthesia by **administering an infusion of tobacco as a sort of enema**.

220 ➤ Don't try this at home

Understandably, some sufferers opted to avoid the physician and attempt do-it-yourself remedies. Founding father Gouverneur Morris, who represented Pennsylvania in the U.S. Constitutional Convention and penned sections of the resulting document, died in 1816 of just such DIY doctoring: Afflicted with a urinary-tract blockage, Morris tried to clear the problem by **inserting a whale-bone in his urethra**.

221 ➤ One treatment is enough for anyone

Because of the high mortality rate associated with surgery, some medical theorists began to promote less-invasive ways of curing, well, just about anything that ailed you—notably **dunking in an ice-water bath**. According to Sir John Floyer, who touted the treatment in the 1700s, the resulting "terror and surprise" would invigorate the patient.

222

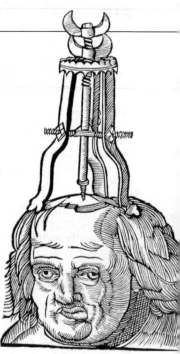

➤ You need this like you need a hole in the head

The "oldest known surgery," trepanning was practiced into the nineteenth century (and continues to have advocates today). Thought to relieve everything from headaches to insanity, trepanning involved slicing the skin of the skull with a sharp knife, pulling back the flaps, and **boring a hole up to two inches in diameter into the skull bone with a device resembling a corkscrew**. About two-thirds of patients actually survived the procedure.

223 ➤ That's change you can believe in
As recently as 1970, Amanda Feilding **bored a hole in her own skull with a dental drill** after failing to find a surgeon who would administer trepanning. She later twice ran for Parliament on a platform calling for Britain's National Health Service to cover the procedure. The first election she got 49 votes; her second try managed 139 votes.

224 ➤ You'll feel a little pinch before the explosion
Rev. Cotton Mather and Dr. Zabdiel Boylston were the first to employ "variolation," a form of vaccination, in America, against a smallpox epidemic that infected half of Boston in 1721. For his troubles, **the reverend's house was firebombed** by people who believed variolation was blasphemy and feared it would actually spread smallpox.

225 ➤ Dying for a glass of OJ
Scurvy, easily prevented if only people had understood the importance of vitamin C, typically **killed half the ship's crew on any lengthy sea voyage.** Between 1500 and 1850, it's estimated two million sailors died from scurvy.

226 ➤ The results are fuzzy
In a pioneering eighteenth-century experiment, James Lind showed that sailors fed oranges and limes recovered from scurvy. Despite his findings, however, **Lind remained convinced that scurvy was caused by toxins from inadequately digested food.**

227 ➤ Tea-ing it up
Tea was once thought so important to proper bowel functioning that **one physician recommended drinking at least fifty cups of tea a day.** Extreme cases called for up to two hundred cups daily.

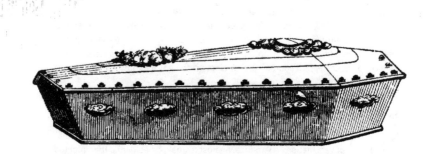

228 ➤ Have you considered a career in grave robbing?

The proliferation of medical schools and a drop in the rate of executions led to **an epidemic of body snatching** in the seventeenth and eighteenth centuries. Lacking proper refrigeration, cadavers for the study of anatomy didn't last long, so the demand for fresh corpses was constant. Besides, the body-snatching business was profitable and the punishment for those who were caught was often only a fine; in Britain, it wasn't even a criminal offense until passage of the 1832 Anatomy Act.

229 ➤ That's a fine way to pay your respects

Body snatchers, archly dubbed "resurrectionists," typically worked in teams and preferred fresh graves, which required less spadework to dig up their occupants. Women who worked for the resurrectionists would **go to funerals to spy out candidates for body-snatching**.

230 ➤ The price of resting in peace

Bereaved relatives, fearful of having their loved ones' corpses stolen for medical research, took extreme methods to secure the coffins. These security measures included coffins made of iron, **alarms attached to graves, and the Mortsafe, a structure of iron bars constructed around a coffin.**

231 ➤ Easy pickings

As security measures made it more difficult to rob the graves of the well-to-do, paupers' mass graves became a favorite target of "resurrectionists." Sometimes the **coffins were simply stacked until the graves were full**, making easy pickings for those snatching bodies for medical schools.

232 ➤ If I die before I wake...

On the bright side, if your body got snatched, at least you'd have a chance to escape being buried alive, which was a peculiarly feared fixation in the nineteenth century—likely because of **the inability of medical practitioners to tell when someone was truly dead**. Wilkie Collins, the novelist who wrote *The Moonstone*, also penned detailed instructions posted at his bedside every night for double-checking in case he'd apparently died in his sleep.

233 ➤ It really wasn't their time

Apparently the Victorian era's fear of being buried alive was not entirely imagined. One report of bodies exhumed for various reasons in New York City between 1860 and 1880 showed that six of the 1,200 bodies showed signs of "post-interment distress," such as **thrashing or scratching within the coffin.**

234 ➤ This meeting ends over our cold, dead bodies

Whole organizations sprang up to battle the supposed scourge of premature burial. **The Society for the Prevention of People Being Buried Alive** was founded in the United States in 1896, following the establishment of the Association for the Prevention of Premature Burial in London.

235 ➤ Break coffin in case of an emergency

The fear of being pronounced dead prematurely by an incompetent doctor led to elaborate burial precautions, including **placing crowbars and shovels in caskets so victims could dig their way out**. Some coffins contained a pipe that occupants who woke up could use for air and to holler for help to servants posted by fresh graves.

236 ➤ Why take any chances?

On the other hand, just to make certain people thought dead stayed that way, some **caskets were fitted with poison gas** that was released when the box was sealed.

237 ➤ Cutting one's teeth

We're not sure if this is how George Washington got his famous wooden teeth, but back then it wasn't uncommon to order false teeth by mail. To ensure a (relatively) good fit, the patient would **bite into a piece of soft wood to make tooth marks** and measure his gums with a length of ribbon.

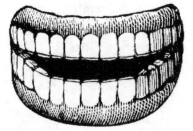

238 ➤ You have his smile
Besides wood, false teeth could be made of bone, ivory, agate or even of **teeth previously belonging to another person**.

239 ➤ A different kind of lockjaw
Wooden false teeth didn't always fit very well, especially if you needed both upper and bottom dentures. To synchronize top and bottom false teeth when the mouth opened, denture makers sometimes attached a metal spring in the back. The springs had to be quite tight, so **closing your mouth once it was open could prove a bit of a challenge** and required powerful jaw muscles.

240 ➤ It was a shocking scene
The eighteenth-century discovery that electricity could make the legs of frogs—even dead ones—twitch soon led to some gruesome medical demonstrations. In stage shows, **electricity was used to "animate" human corpses**, such as the bodies of executed murderers.

241 ➤ Moving like greased lightning
It was a small logical leap from juicing up corpses to treating what ails you with the magic of electricity. Soon, **electricity was used for everything from "curing" constipation** to "treating" young men with randy impulses.

242 ➤ A smile that lights up the room
Guillaume Duchenne, a nineteenth-century neurology researcher, attempted to map all the body's nerves and muscles by zapping people with electricity. He became particularly fascinated with the face, which he could contort to order by electrical stimulation—sometimes, for example, causing the left side of a face to show an expression while leaving the right side unzapped. **Duchenne was frustrated, however, in his attempts to stimulate a true smile with electrodes.** A genuine, perfect smile is today sometimes called a "Duchenne smile"—no zapping required.

243 ➤ A matter of degrees

What's "normal" body temperature? The popular figure of 98.6 degrees Fahrenheit was set by a German doctor, Carl Wunderlich, after more than a million readings of 25,000 patients, in 1861. **But 98.6 was wrong.** Not until 1992 did a study find that "normal" actually ranges from 96 to 99.9 degrees, with an average of 98.2.

244 ➤ We hope the waiting room had good magazines...

Sir Thomas Clifford Allbut developed the modern clinical thermometer in 1866. Prior to Allbut's invention, it required **20 minutes to take a person's temperature**.

245 ➤ Does this look infected to you?

When President James A. Garfield was shot in 1881, he might have survived the assassination attempt if not for his doctors. For eleven agonizing weeks, **doctors probed his bullet wounds with their unsterilized hands**, creating "enormous tunnels of pus" throughout Garfield's body.

246 ➤ How's that go? Feed a bullet wound...

Adding to Garfield's agony, a physician with the unlikely name of Dr. Doctor Willard Bliss insisted on **stuffing the wounded president with heavy meals and alcohol**, which triggered bouts of vomiting.

247 ➤ No transcripts? No problem

As recently as 1900, **only one U.S. medical school required incoming students to have a college degree**, and no more than twenty demanded even a high-school diploma. Academic training in science? Not necessary—as long as you could pay the tuition.

248 ➤ Pretty deadly

In 1904, Marie Curie boasted that **radiation would prolong life**. She would sometimes carry test tubes of radioactive isotopes around in her pocket or keep them in a desk drawer, and admired the pretty blue-green light emitted by radioactive substances. The two-time Nobel prizewinner would die in 1934 of leukemia from overexposure to radiation.

249 ➤ Have you had your flu shot?

Epidemiologists today estimate that **the 1918 influenza killed fifty to one hundred million people worldwide**—more than the Black Death of the Middle Ages killed in a century. The 1918 pandemic claimed more victims in twenty-four weeks than AIDS in twenty-four years. Some historians believe more soldiers died from the flu than from all the battles of World War I.

250 ➤ Good thing she wasn't waiting for pizza delivery...

The 1918–19 flu epidemic was notable for its speed. In Washington, D.C., one young woman called authorities to report that two of her roommates were dead and another sick, while she alone remained uninfected. **By the time officials reached the apartment, all four women were dead.**

251 ➤ Bottom floor, the afterlife

In another example of the swiftness of the "Spanish flu," the operator of a mine elevator was stricken by a "sweating paralysis" so quickly that there was no time to evacuate the elevator before he lost control. **The elevator plunged to the bottom of the mine shaft, killing twenty-four miners**—collateral damage from the flu.

252 ➤ The spitting image of a lawbreaker

In New York City, desperate efforts to stop the spread of the flu epidemic included a ban on spitting in public; **five hundred illegal spitters were arrested**.

253 ➤ Leading to the invention of the "air kiss"

During the 1918 flu epidemic, New York City's health commissioner urged people to **kiss through a handkerchief to avoid spreading infection**.

254 ➤ Imagine ripping that off quickly

The original Band-Aid adhesive bandage, introduced in 1920, was a flop, selling only three thousand dollars' worth in the first year. No wonder: **The bandages were made by hand, three inches wide and eighteen inches long**. Not until smaller and easier-to-use bandages were shipped overseas as part of the war effort in 1942 did the familiar Band-Aid begin to catch on.

255 ➤ High times

Imports of opium to the United States—for "medicinal" purposes—soared from 24,000 pounds in 1840 to at least **400,000 pounds of opium a year by 1872**.

256 ⤙ The monkey on Uncle Sam's back

Morphine, derived from opium and first synthesized in 1803, was so popular a drug for treating the pain of injured Civil War soldiers that **morphine addiction became known as "the army disease."** Nearly thirteen million opium pills and other opium preparations were dispensed to Union soldiers.

257 ⤙ Tough choice

Physicians who tended to Civil War soldiers might ask, "How are your bowels?" **Soldiers who were constipated got mercury**; those whose bowels were "open" rather than "closed" were dispensed opium for their diarrhea.

258 ⤙ I'd like to order a spinning wheel and some opium

Opiates remained popular long after the Civil War, as ingredients in patent medicines. You could **order opium-containing concoctions,** such as laudanum and Paregoric, through the Sears, Roebuck mail-order catalog.

259 ⤙ Don't forget your paraphernalia

As a convenience to the growing number of morphine addicts, **Sears also carried hypodermic syringes in its mail-order catalogs.** Perfected in 1853, the syringe was thought to be a less-addictive method of administering morphine than orally.

260 ➤ One dose for junior, one for mom

Although women were the chief consumers of opium, they also gave it to their children. **Opium was thought to be good for croup.**

261 ➤ Your baby is so quiet!

Even young children's medications in the 1880s—products like Kopp's Baby Friend and Winslow's Soothing Syrup—**contained addictive amounts of morphine.**

262 ➤ One tablespoon cough syrup, shaken not stirred

At 30 to 40 percent alcohol, patent **medicines packed as much alcohol in a single spoonful as a full cocktail.** Some estimated that Americans in the 1870s and 1880s got more alcohol from medications than from liquor.

263 ➤ Tell me, how does this make you feel?

Sigmund Freud, the famed father of psychoanalysis, not only used cocaine himself—he endorsed it for its therapeutic benefits. In an 1884 paper, "On Coca," **Freud wrote enthusiastically about cocaine's clinical benefits and "the most gorgeous excitement" the drug induced.** Much of the evidence he cited was lifted from a magazine published by a pharmaceutical firm that sold cocaine.

264 ➤ Things go better with cocaine

A friend of Freud's, Viennese surgeon Carl Koller, did the most to **popularize cocaine in the medical world as an anesthetic.** When cocaine was ingested orally, Koller observed, it numbed the tongue.

265 ➤ Numb, but nuts

Given the lack of anesthetic options in the 1880s, cocaine quickly caught on—until cases of "cocaine psychosis" began to be reported, in which **patients might hallucinate that snakes were crawling all over their bodies.**

266 ➤ Crazy is as crazy does

If you weren't already crazy, being sent to a nineteenth-century asylum would make you that way—if you survived. An 1878 report on conditions in New Jersey' state asylum found that **"treatments" included being starved, dunked in frigid water, and soaked and then locked outside in winter weather.**

267 ➤ Nope, he's not faking

To make sure patients weren't faking epileptic symptoms, asylum staff sometimes **dowsed patients in alcohol and set them on fire.**

268 ➤ Who's the crazy one here?

Before the development of modern antipsychotic medications, almost everything was tried to treat psychiatric patients—most notably lobotomies. António Egas Moniz actually shared the Nobel Prize in medicine in 1949 for his "discovery of the therapeutic value" of the procedure. Originally, Moniz tried drilling holes in a patient's skull and injecting alcohol to destroy tissue in the brain's frontal lobes. He later switched to **cutting out brain tissue using a rotating, retractable wire loop**. Although the procedure was later largely abandoned, Moniz's Nobel Prize has never been withdrawn.

269 ➤ A chip off the old noggin

By 1951, almost twenty thousand lobotomies had been performed in the United States. Refinements to the procedure included Dr. Walter Freeman's **"ice-pick lobotomy,"** in which a mallet was used to drive a sharp instrument through the thin layer of bone at the top of the eye socket and into the brain. Freeman developed the technique using an ice pick from his own kitchen on grapefruit and cadavers.

270 ➤ Nurse Ratched, stat!

Although today "electroshock therapy" (now called electroconvulsive therapy or ECT) is, with the patient's informed consent, considered an accepted treatment for psychiatric and other conditions, its history was sometimes, well, shocking. Early experiments produced memory loss and confusion. In the 1940s, **psychiatrists tried curare, the muscle-paralyzing South American poison, to modify the convulsions**.

271 ➤ A very, very deep sleep

Other experimenters with electroshock combined the treatment with barbiturates, putting patients in a deep sleep for several days. This procedure **killed twenty-six Australian patients**.

272 ➤ Coma time, again?

From 1933 until the 1970s, schizophrenia patients were sometimes given insulin coma therapy, in which **massive doses of insulin were administered to induce daily, hour-long comas**. Evidence for the therapy's success was largely anecdotal and probably skewed by the selection of patients, who were given special privileges when not comatose. Asked to explain the uncritical acceptance of the therapy, one expert ventured, "It meant that psychiatrists had something to do. It made them feel like real doctors instead of just institutional attendants." One U.S. survivor of fifty forced insulin coma treatments combined with electroshock described it as "the most devastating, painful and humiliating experience of my life ... a flat-out atrocity."

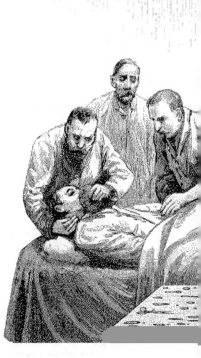

273 ➤ Somebody skipped Ethics 101

In the infamous "Tuskegee experiment," the U.S. Public Health Service studied the progression of syphilis among 399 impoverished African American sharecroppers from Macon County, Alabama, from 1932 to 1972, along with 201 control subjects without the disease. **The men were never told they had syphilis**—their condition was instead described as "bad blood"—or treated for the disease, even though in the 1940s penicillin was proven to be a cure for syphilis.

274 ➤ Strangled by science

Thomas Midgley Jr., best known as the inventor of ozone-depleting chlorofluoro-carbons as well as the lead additive in gasoline, was stricken with polio at age fifty-one and turned his attention to medical inventions. Midgley developed an elaborate system of pulleys and wires that could lift a crippled patient from bed. In 1944, at age fifty-five, however, **he became entangled in his own contraption and died of strangulation**.

275 ➤ Was this the inspiration for *Tremors*?

Early pregnancy tests included **sprinkling sulfur on a woman's urine** to see if it would then breed worms.

276 ➤ Your specialty is what exactly, doctor?

Some physicians, who became known as "**piss prophets**," claimed to be able to determine if a woman was pregnant by the color of her urine or by mixing wine with the urine.

277 ➤ The blue lines are easier to read

The "rabbit test," developed in 1928 originally using mice, actually relied on the presence of a hormone in a pregnant woman's urine. If a woman was pregnant, injecting her urine into a female rabbit caused it to ovulate. The popular phrase, "The rabbit died"—meaning the woman was pregnant—was misleading because **the rabbit *always* died**, as it had to be killed to see the results.

278 ➤ Croak once for yes

Tired of killing rabbits, scientists also imported African clawed frogs to use in pregnancy testing. Unfortunately, the **frogs brought with them a fungal disease that escaped the lab** and now threatens many amphibian species.

279 ➤ Honey, we're going to need more sheep's blood

The first home-pregnancy test, introduced in 1978, included a test-tube stand with a mirror at the bottom that women had to use to observe patterns in the tube, plus **a batch of solutions, including sheep's blood.**

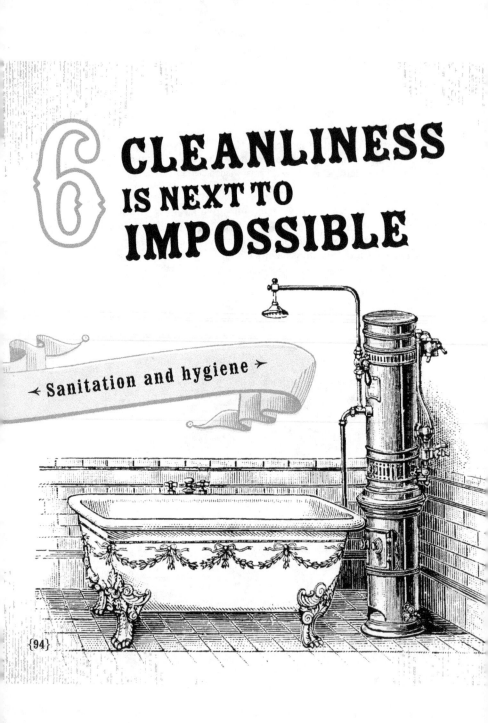

6 CLEANLINESS IS NEXT TO IMPOSSIBLE

Sanitation and hygiene

280

➤ Look out below!

Early toilets took all sorts of forms, from the "necessary chair" to chamber pots. If nothing else was handy, **people might urinate in flower vases or simply out the nearest window.**

281 ➤ A litter box for men

In the early nineteenth century, gentlemen in particular might keep a crude sort of **"earth closet"** (as opposed to the "water closet") in their billiard rooms or hunting parlors. Rather than water, these privies contained dirt or ashes that could be scraped over the results of relieving yourself.

282 ➤ A dirty business

A more refined "earth closet" was patented in 1860 by the Reverend Henry Moule. The vicar's invention worked much like a flush toilet, except that when the handle was pulled, **a measured amount of dry dirt would be released** from a storage tank to cover up the sight and smell of what was in the toilet.

283 ➤ You're going to need a stronger air freshener

Even when toilets began flushing with water that actually washed away the contents, the system was far from foolproof. Until the invention of the water trap and U-bend that kept a small water reservoir between the user and the sewers, every time a person flushed, **the toilet opened to the odors and sewage that lay beneath.**

284 ➤ But how did the corn crops fare?

The discovery of the benefits of bat guano as fertilizer in the 1830s had one un-fortunate side effect, depending on your point of view: The bottom fell out, so to speak, of **the market for human waste as fertilizer**. No longer able to peddle their populace's waste to farmers, cities soon faced a messy sewage crisis.

285 ➤ What goes in must come out

The rapid population growth in cities contributed to an excrement explosion. By the 1830s, the population of fast-growing New York City added an estimated **one hundred tons or more of excrement to cesspits every day**. Often these crude sewage repositories were dangerously close to wells and other water sources, making the water all but undrinkable and contributing to a cholera epidemic that struck the city in 1832.

286 ➤ Don't look under their fingernails

Before there was toilet paper, **almost anything might be employed for personal cleaning**: stones, pieces of clay, sponges on sticks, mussel shells, fur and, for the right-handed, the left hand. This may have contributed to prejudice against left-handedness.

287 ➤ No corn on the cob for me, thanks

In rural America, the outhouse typically was equipped with a box of corncobs or, in less persnickety homesteads, **a corncob hung on a string**—meant to be reused.

288 ➤ TP or not TP, that is the question…

The invention of toilet paper was a blow to poetry sales. Previously, part of the education of a young English gentleman involved buying an inexpensive volume or two of verse to peruse while doing one's business in the bathroom. When finished, **the pages one had already read could be torn out of the book and used for personal hygiene.**

289

➤ Pa! I was gonna order from that page!

Toilet paper as we enjoy it today, rolled and perforated, was introduced in the late 1870s. But it was slow to reach more rural regions, **who thriftily made use instead of the Sears, Roebuck and Co. catalog.** Little did Richard Sears imagine how literally customers would interpret the slogans on the cover of his 1894 catalog, which declared it the "Book of Bargains: A Money Saver for Everyone" and the "Cheapest Supply House on Earth." America's outhouses were never quite the same after Sears introduced nonabsorbent-coated stock in the catalog for color pictures.

290 ➤ Your smile looks a little ashy

At the time of the invention of the toothbrush, in 1780, **the popular method of cleaning one's teeth involved rubbing with a rag dipped in salt and soot.**

291 ➤ The toothbrush's checkered past

It took some time in prison—always a fine place for inventors to think—for English-man William Addis to come up with a better way to clean one's teeth: **He drilled some holes in an animal bone and threaded them with pig bristles** begged from a guard. (Later pricey toothbrushes used badger hair for the brush.) After getting out of stir, Addis turned his toothbrushes into a profitable business, which still operates today as Wisdom Toothbrushes.

292 ➤ The original Old Spice

Although commercial deodorants didn't come along until "Mum" in 1888, humans have been trying to cover up our odor since at least ancient Egypt. **The Egyptians tried daubing their armpits with spices and citrus oils.** They also came up with the innovation of trimming underarm hair to reduce the smelly surface area.

293 ➤ Eau de billy goat

Early deodorants were imperfect at best: The author Ovid once complained that many of his fellow **Roman men smelled as though they were carrying goats under their arms**.

294 ➤ Were they hydrophobic?

In the eighteenth century, **most people turned up their noses at the notion of washing with water.** Many opted instead for "dry washing," vigorously scrubbing their bodies with a brush.

295 ➤ Let's hope they were quick baths

Benjamin Franklin argued instead for "air baths," and frequently scandalized the neighbors by **walking around naked outside** to air out his body.

296 ➤ It's a start, but not enough

Others simply believed that **changing their clothes would get rid of bodily grime.** Linen, in particular, was thought to have dirt-absorbing powers.

297

➤ Tighty not-so-whiteys

The introduction of underwear was a boon to cleanliness in the era before bathing became popular, because **the grime on people's bodies would rub off** (at least a little) onto their undergarments. The underwear could then be washed, even if its wearers declined to bathe.

298 ➤ The path to heaven is paved with clean shirts

Methodism founder John Wesley coined the phrase "cleanliness is next to godliness" in a 1778, but that hardly made him an early advocate of bathing. Rather, Wesley was **preaching about the importance of clean clothes**. As for the body underneath, he thought believers could make do with an occasional foot wash and regular shaving of the face.

299 ➤ A shower three decades in the making

Even into the nineteenth century, bathing was an oddity, engaged in—if at all—more for quack therapeutic purposes than for cleanliness. Elizabeth Drinker, wife of a prominent Quaker in Philadelphia, had a showering apparatus installed in her backyard in 1799, and said of the experience, "I bore it better than expected, **not having been wet all over at once for twenty-eight years past**."

300 ➤ All those opposed to bathing say "Aye"

Some nineteenth-century officials viewed bathing not as therapy but as a health hazard: In Philadelphia in 1835, the Common Council missed by only two votes passing a ban on wintertime bathing; in 1845, **Boston banned bathing** except when prescribed by a doctor.

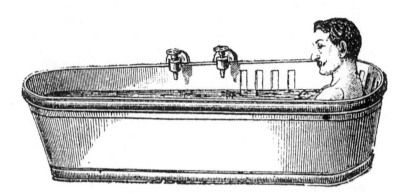

301 ➤ But I just bathed last week

In frontier America, **"bath night" remained a weekly ritual at best**, involving heating buckets of water on the woodstove. In *Farmer Boy*, Laura Ingalls Wilder recalled of her future husband, "Almanzo ... didn't like Saturday night. On Saturday night there was no cozy evening by the heater, with apples, popcorn and cider. Saturday night was bath night."

302 ➤ Honey, where's my shower helmet?

Once the Victorians finally discovered baths and showers, they went at it with a penitential fury. Cold baths—the colder, the better—were preferred, and shower heads were designed to deliver a needle-like pounding. Before you dared get into some showers, **you had to don protective headgear to keep from being knocked unconscious by the force of the water**.

303 ➤ It's a good way to get to know other guests

Even in posh hotels, indoor plumbing remained a rare luxury and guests had to trudge to the outhouse or share a bathroom down the hall. The Mount Vernon Hotel in Cape May, New Jersey, was the first such establishment in the world to offer a private bathroom for every guest room. Claiming to be the world's largest hotel, at 432 rooms, and equipped with a water tank holding twenty thousand gallons, the Mount Vernon opened in 1853 but was still completing construction when it burned to the ground in 1856. Perhaps fearing a similar fate, or seeing how much such bathroom extravagance had cost, **no other hotel splurged on private baths for every guest until after the turn of the century**.

304 ➤ Don't stop and smell the students

Schools were among the early adopters of the notion that people, even children, needed to bathe once in a while. But teachers often met parental resistance. When one teacher sent home a note suggesting that young Willie get a bath, the reply came: **"Willie ain't a flower, he is a boy; learn him, don't smell him."**

305 ➤ The great unwashed

Enterprising cities, desperate to clean up their unwashed populace, began **opening public bathhouses**. By 1908, Philadelphia boasted fifteen public baths. Milwaukee bathed some 600,000 people a year, at a cost per person of 2.5 cents.

306

➤ Flunking the Armhole Odor Test

Though people had been stinking for millennia, the term "B.O." didn't appear until a 1919 ad. A deodorant for women with the awkward, but memorable, name of Odo-Ro-No was the first company to use the abbreviation "B.O." (but not the actual words, "body odor"). Previously, deodorant marketers had confined their pitch to suggestions about how they would foster daintiness and sweetness. But Odo-Ro-No took a more direct approach, with ads advising consumers to take the "Armhole Odor Test" and warning that **social success hinged on eliminating B.O.** If you didn't use Odo-Ro-No, ads warned women, you'd be "always a bridesmaid, never a bride."

307 ➤ Could they at least let the ladies in on the secret?

The first commercial women's sanitary pads, introduced by Johnson & Johnson in 1896, were Lister's Towels. They sold poorly, however, since **advertising for such products was considered improper**. When Kimberly-Clark introduced Kotex in 1920, it created a separate division for the product so its image wouldn't be sullied.

308 ➤ Rolling your own

Tampons didn't become commercially available until the 1930s and didn't gain acceptance until Tampax in 1936. Before then, women improvised, **making their own from surgical cotton or adapting natural sponges** bought at art-supply stores.

309 ➤ Give us back our market share

Church groups and physicians initially expressed reservations about the newfangled store-bought tampon. For doctors, this opposition was "a curious reversal," according to a 1945 article in the *Journal of the American Medical Association*: **They had been selling female patients medical tampons for years**, and "the tampon used to pay the office rent."

310 ➤ Letting off some steam at night

While diffident at best about bathing, people in the nineteenth century were obsessed with the imagined horrors of impurities in the air they breathed out and that they exuded from their skin—especially at night. Twin beds were thus recommended for married couples, not only to prevent accidental intimacy but to protect against "**the poisonous substances which have escaped through the pores of the skin.**" One supposed expert calculated that as many as 40 percent of deaths in the United States could be blamed on the poisonous fumes somehow present when people were asleep.

311 ➤ Rats!

Rats continued to be a worry long after the Black Death and plagues were history. As recently as 1944, *The New Yorker* recounted how exterminators working one **posh Manhattan hotel rounded up 236 rats in just three nights**. In New York City offices, secretaries reported rats popping out of their desk drawers.

312 ➤ This city has gone to the hogs

The first New York City street cleaners were pigs—literally. So filthy was the fast-growing city that **herds of pigs were pressed into service to scavenge the ever-mounting trash**. In 1842, after Charles Dickens paid a visit to New York City, he penned a warning to future tourists: "Take care of the pigs. Two portly sows are trotting up behind this carriage, and a select party of half a dozen gentlemen hogs have just now turned the corner.... They are the city scavengers, these pigs."

313 ➤ Business is picking up

Even after New York City caught on to the idea of garbage collection, not every American metropolis invested as heavily in picking up after its citizens. By 1906, **New York City was spending $1.50 per person per year on garbage disposal**; St. Louis spent just 12 cents a head and Cleveland, 18 cents. Up in Buffalo, New York, the annual garbage tab was still less than a nickel per person.

314 ➤ Pigging out

New York City wasn't the only town where hogs were an everyday sight. In Cincinnati, nicknamed "Porkopolis" for its hog-butchering operations, **half a million pigs were herded through the streets to the city's fifty slaughterhouses every year** in the 1860s.

315 ➤ Horse puckey!

In 1900, New York City was home to 150,000 horses, which produced more than **three million pounds of manure a day**.

316 ➤ What a pile of...

Upstate, in Rochester, New York, at the start of the twentieth century, the city's horses pumped out **enough manure to cover an acre of ground with a pile 175 feet high**.

317 ➤ Maybe they should look into guard rails

The smoggy gloom of coal fires was so thick in Victorian London that people often walked right into walls even in the middle of the day. On one particularly poor-visibility day, **seven pedestrians in a row walked right into the Thames**, falling into the river one after another.

318 ➤ On the bright side (if only you could see it...)

People learned to live with pollution, even rationalizing it as a sign of prosperity. **Some doctors argued that smoky air was actually good for you**, a preventive against malaria and a cure for "lung and cutaneous diseases."

319 ➤ Not exactly stainless steel

Pittsburgh, famously described by Frank Lloyd Wright as "hell with the lid off," boasted fourteen thousand smokestacks as early as 1900. Local officials estimated the Steel City **residents spent an extra $2.25 million on laundry and other cleaning because of the soot** that filled the air, night and day.

320 ➤ Up in smoke

Until 1954, Los Angeles got rid of its trash the old-fashioned way—by burning it. With no regular trash pickup, **every house and apartment building had its own incinerator**, from which the smell of burning trash wafted every night. No wonder the city was notorious for its smog.

321 ➤ Just stack him over there with the others

Before cemeteries replaced churchyards, burials were a profitable business for many houses of worship. One Baptist chapel, when it ran out of room outdoors, managed to **stuff twelve thousand corpses into its basement in a nineteen-year span**. The stench of rotting bodies from down below seriously cut into attendance at church services.

322 ➤ Six feet under? You're lucky to get six inches

In the nineteenth century, churchyard burial grounds grew **so crowded that it proved challenging to find fresh spots to dig**, for fear of previous corpses' body parts or coffins coming up when the gravedigger stuck in the shovel.

323 ➤ Bring your Bible and your nose plugs

The **smell of churchyards filling up with layer after layer of corpses** became so unpleasant—if not downright dangerous—that the tradition of the bereaved attending grave-side services was often abandoned.

324 ➤ Full of gas, even at the end

Experienced grave diggers knew to drill a hole into a coffin that was being disturbed to make room for new arrivals. **A tube was then inserted to draw off the gases from putrefaction,** which would be burned off to make the coffin safe for handling. "To inhale this gas, undiluted with atmospheric air, is instant death," noted the report of an inquiry into graveyard dangers.

325 ➤ Better dead than Red? Not really...

Burial was especially grim for the poor, as described in horrific detail by Friedrich Engels based on his observations in the 1840s. It's no wonder he went on to be one of the founders of Communism: "The corpses of the poor have no better fate than the carcasses of animals," Engels wrote, describing the pauper burial ground at one church as "a piece of open marshland" where there were **"heaps of bones all over the place."** Engels went on, "Every Wednesday the remains of dead paupers are thrown into a hole which is fourteen feet deep. A clergyman gabbles through the burial service and then the grave is filled with loose soil. On the following Wednesday the ground is opened again and this goes on until it is completely full. The whole neighbourhood is infected by the dreadful stench from this burial ground."

326 ✦ Nice to see you again, Grand-père!

Residents of New Orleans quickly found that burying dead bodies in a city that's below sea level can be tricky. Cemeteries took to weighting down caskets with rocks on top, but **when coffins were made airtight they would rise to the surface.**

327 ✦ Reason to sing the blues

Yellow fever, popularly associated with the tropics, also took its toll on the United States—as far north as Memphis, where **a devastating yellow-fever epidemic in 1878 killed more than five thousand people.** Those who could fled the city, reducing Memphis' population by half. Many of the dead were not found until long afterward, when "the stench of decaying flesh" led to the discovery of their bodies.

328 ✦ H2-Oh!

A torrential rainstorm in 1885 dumped more than five inches of rain on Chicago, literally swamping the city's inadequate sewage system, which simply emptied into the Chicago River. **The storm pushed sewage well out into Lake Michigan, which was the city's source of fresh water.** Only providential rains from the northeast, according to some accounts, kept the sewage out of the intake two miles offshore and prevented a typhoid epidemic.

329 ➤ Her secret ingredient ... typhoid!

Nothing, however, could stop "Typhoid Mary"—a heavyset Irish cook named Mary Mallon—who went from household to household in New York in the early 1900s, spreading typhoid fever. Mary seldom bothered to wash her hands—hardly unusual at the time—and so **spread typhoid bacteria with every meal she prepared**. Estimates of the deaths attributed to Typhoid Mary range as high as fifty.

330 ➤ Next time, check references...if they're still alive

Typhoid Mary was finally tracked down and held in a sort of house arrest in a cottage in the Bronx. But you can't keep an infected woman down: Vowing never to work again as a cook, only as a laundress, Mary was released in 1910. She changed her name to Mary Brown and promptly got a job as a cook. **For the next five years, she went from one kitchen to the next, spreading typhoid fever**. Finally, in 1915, an outbreak of twenty-five cases at Sloan Hospital for Women led authorities to Mary, who had abruptly left her job in the hospital kitchen. She spent the remaining twenty-three years of her life in quarantine.

331 ➤ Not doing a body good

Typhoid Mary was hardly alone, however. In 1908, more than **four hundred cases of typhoid fever were traced to a single milkman**, who "went about his business tasting the stoppers of milk cans." Fifty victims died, as did the milkman.

332 ➤ A real head-scratcher

In spreading typhus, **humans got an assist from lice** living—and pooping—on their bodies and in their clothes. In 1909, Charles Nicolle discovered that bathing typhus patients and sterilizing their clothing to eradicate lice could stop the spread of an epidemic.

333 ➤ Fiery itch and brimstone

So omnipresent were lice in America's schools that **children often wore little sacks of powdered brimstone**—thought to ward off lice—around their necks. Brimstone, a type of sulphur, combined with lard was also used as an ointment against the itch from lice bites.

7 HOME IS WHERE THE HORROR IS

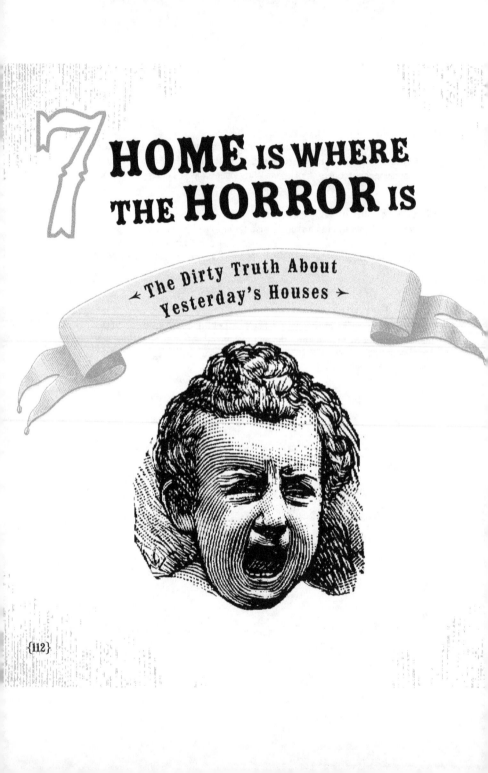

The Dirty Truth About Yesterday's Houses

334 ➤ This may be why shoes were invented

The floors of houses were originally just bare earth covered with dried rushes. Although new rushes might be laid down twice a year, the old ones were simply left underneath. A thick floor was considered a sign of a family's status—and made an ideal **nesting ground for insects, rodents, and plague germs**.

335 ➤ Why is the shirt you need always at the bottom?

The chest of drawers didn't appear until the 1600s, when someone had the bright idea to put, well, drawers into a chest. Prior to that breakthrough, people kept everything they owned in trunks, whose **domed lids helped the rain run off** when the trucks were toted from place to place.

336 ➤ Forget resale value

Early American houses, lacking lime for binding, were little more than huts made of dried mud. **Few houses lasted more than ten years** before falling apart.

337 ➤ If only they had a Home Depot

Adequate stone for building was so scarce in colonial America that **George Washington had to import flagstones all the way from England** to pave his patio.

338 ➤ How hard can it be?

Bricks, an alternative to wood and stone for home-building, weren't as easy to make as you might think. One amateur brick-maker who thought he could master the DIY approach for his own house **fired 150,000 bricks before giving up** and turning to the professionals.

339 ➤ At least the neighbor kids can't break bricks

Taxes on glass in the eighteenth century were so steep that **many people bricked up their windows**. Frames for windows had to be overbuilt to compensate for the thinness and lightness of window glass, which was taxed in part by weight.

340 ➤ Careful with that package

America simply didn't have enough glass for windows at any price in the eighteenth century. People planning to emigrate across the Atlantic were counseled to **bring windows with them**—an uncertain proposition at best on a long sea voyage.

341 ➤ Kind of a tip-off for burglars, though

In colonial times, people who could actually afford windows sometimes had the windows **all removed and stored for safekeeping when they were away** from home, to avoid breakage and theft.

342 ➤ Bugs versus breathing

Open the windows to let in fresh air or close them to keep out bugs? It was a constant issue in early homes, where **everything from silk to cheesecloth was tried as a way of screening open windows.** Wire window screens became available in the eighteenth century, and Thomas Jefferson employed them at Monticello, but the wire mesh had to be fashioned by hand and so remained prohibitively expensive. The industrial manufacture of wire mesh, developed by the Gilbert & Bennett Manufacturing Company of Connecticut in the 1840s, didn't really take off until the Civil War. Then, deprived of customers in the Confederacy, the company tried other uses for its mesh—among them, window screens.

343 ➤ Long before IKEA

The term "board," as in "room and board," comes from the **planks that were laid across trestles to form primitive dining-room tables.**

344 ➤ Making a toast took forever!

Glassware was scarce in early dining rooms, so guests didn't always get a drinking vessel to call their own: Sometimes you had to **share your glass with the person eating next to you.**

345 ➤ A dishwasher? We'd settle for a sink

Although a fancy meal in the mid-nineteenth century might **dirty nearly five hundred dishes,** most kitchens did not have a sink. All those dishes and pots would have to be toted to a separate room to be scrubbed, then hauled back to their cupboards.

346 ➤ Mind the sparks, luv

Although the development of brick chimneys cleared the air in houses, which previously had been filled with a haze of smoke, people complained that the newfangled fireplaces, vented to the outside, never got the inside of houses warm enough. A sort of arms race ensued, in which fireplaces were built ever bigger to make them produce adequate heat. Eventually, some **fireplaces were so large that they could accommodate benches inside by the fire**, where at least residents could sit and be warm.

347 ➤ We hold these truths ... dang, frozen again!

No matter how you stoked the fire, some winter nights it remained bitterly cold inside. Thomas Jefferson once noted that he had to stop writing one night because **the ink for his pen kept freezing**.

348 ➤ Throw another log on the fire, and another

Keeping homes in early America warm meant denuding the local landscape. A typical house burned through as much as twenty cords of firewood a year. One Long Island village reportedly **chopped down every stick of wood as far as the eye could see** within fourteen years of the town's founding.

349 ➤ Coal or cold

Coal eventually began to replace firewood for heating middle-class homes, but it still took a lot of fuel to keep a house warm. **One home could burn through a ton of coal per month** in cold weather.

350 ➤ All that manual labor will warm you up, too

Not that the development of the coal-fired stove made keeping warm easy. The Boston School of Housekeeping calculated in 1899 that **the typical coal stove required fifty-four minutes a day of cleaning and maintenance**, from emptying the ashes to polishing.

351 ➤ Who needs to see out, anyway?

Early gas heating was no better. In a 1908 book, *The Cost of Cleanness*, Ellen Henrietta Richards calculated that 1,400 hours a year of special heavy cleaning were required for a standard eight-room house heated by gas. **Washing windows dirtied by gas took 120 hours a year** alone.

352 ➤ Better to curse the darkness, after all

Light was as elusive as warmth for our ancestors. Tallow candles, although less pricey than beeswax, produced as much odor as they did uneven, flickering light, and had to be **trimmed as much as forty times an hour**.

353 ➤ An excuse for going to bed early

Oil lamps required almost as much maintenance as tallow candles, including daily cleaning. **By bedtime, an oil lamp might have lost nearly half its illuminating power** to the accumulation of a single night's soot.

354 ➤ Call me Ishmael!

Let's not forget that the best oil for household lamps came from whales. Estimates vary, but one guess is that **300,000 whales were slaughtered between 1830 and 1870 in order to keep lamps lit.**

355 ➤ A yellow thumb

Kerosene and gas replaced whale oil and probably saved the sperm whale from extinction. But they had problems, too: Gas lights left a sooty residue everywhere, blackened ceilings, corroded metal, and even **wilted and yellowed indoor plants.**

356 ➤ Dang gas company!

Lighting a gas lamp was tricky, especially because gas companies typically reduced the flow during the day when demand was less. To get a lamp lit during the day, therefore, meant turning up the gas—creating potentially **a nasty surprise later when the gas flow was boosted back** to normal.

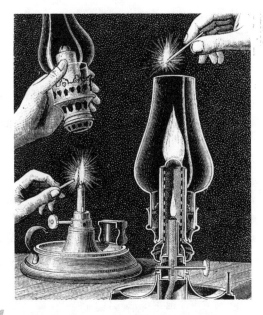

357

➤ **Explosions are so hard to read by**

Kerosene, which was routinely used for household lighting, was "as explosive as gunpowder." Authorities in 1880
estimated that nearly **40 percent of all fires in New
York City could be blamed on kerosene lamps**.

---

358 ➤ Tight quarters

In the early 1870s, it was estimated that almost **half the population of New
York City—about a half-million people—lived in slums**. A family of eight
might be crammed into a two-room tenement apartment measuring some 170
square feet.

359 ➤ That's why they call them slum LORDS

Tenement living was far from cheap. Figured per square foot, **slumlords charged
25 to 35 percent more** than did landlords of fashionable uptown apartments.

360 ➤ Out on the street

Of course, many people counted themselves lucky just to have a home. In New York City, where landlords could evict tenants without any sort of official hearing, **more than forty-three thousand renters were evicted in 1884 alone** for falling behind on their rent.

361

➤ Hot enough for ya?

Life before air-conditioning could be worse than uncomfortable—in a heat wave, it could be fatal. **An 1896 heat wave in New York City led to three thousand deaths.** Many slum-dwelling families endured the heat in windowless inside rooms—supposedly banned in New York City by an 1879 ordinance. Landlords installed airshafts to get around the rule, but these shafts were used as garbage chutes, adding stench instead of outside air.

362 ➤ Green with poison

Early on, wallpaper could make you sick or even kill you. It contained toxic metals, such as lead, arsenic, and antimony. In about 1770, Swedish chemist Carl Scheele "improved" wallpaper with the invention of a coloring pigment so popular that soon "Scheele's Green" was in homes everywhere. The only problem was that the pigment contained copper arsenite, which could become deadly if the wallpaper got wet and moldy. Mold converted the compound to a vapor form of arsenic that is highly poisonous. It's been speculated that **Napoleon, thought to have died of arsenic poisoning, might have been killed by green wallpaper.**

363 ➤ Arsenic and old lace

Scheele's Green was too bright a hue for some uses, so another chemical was added to create an emerald green—copper acetate. The resulting **arsenic-laced pigment could be found all around the house in the nineteenth century**, from candles to curtains.

364 ➤ It needs another coat of poison

Not that painted walls were much safer, as most paints beginning in the nineteenth century contained lead. **Lead poisoning was an unknown occupational hazard for painters, who often developed "painter's colic."**

365 ➤ Paint versus children, that's a toughie

Not until 1897 did scientists begin to suspect a link between lead in paint and childhood lead poisoning. Most European countries banned interior lead paints by 1922, but **the United States didn't pass legislation banning the deadly paint until 1971,** and the ban was not complete until 1978.

366 ➤ The room looks lovely in charred black

A further hazard of getting your house painted was linseed oil, essential to making the pigments in paint harden into a thin sheet. Made from flax seeds, linseed oil is extremely flammable—**an open container of linseed oil would sometimes spontaneously combust**. Many homeowners got a house fire instead of a freshly painted drawing room.

367 ➤ Op art, before its time

The ready commercial availability of interior paint sometimes outstripped what might be considered good taste. In the late eighteenth century, so taken were homeowners with the possibilities of paint that they would apply a **half-dozen or more bright colors—the brighter and bolder the better!—on the walls of a single room**.

368 ➤ A chore the geese were none too fond of, either

Including the mattress, pillows, and bolsters, a feather bed might contain as much as **eighty pounds of feathers, all of which had to be aired out or changed entirely several times a year because they began to stink**. Some families kept whole flocks of geese just for the purpose of plucking them for fresh bed stuffing.

369 ➤ The mattress is looking a little shaggy

If you couldn't afford feathers, other materials used to stuff mattresses included **straw, sawdust, wood shavings, hair (human or horse), dried corn-husks,** and even sea moss.

370 ➤ Sleep tight

The phrase "sleep tight" originated with the need to **rearrange the ropes that held a mattress in place on the bed frame**. The tightly woven ropes, laced in a lattice pattern, would stretch and sag with use and had to be periodically tightened.

371 ⊱ Don't let the bedbugs bite

Brass beds became fashionable in the nineteenth century not because they were nice and shiny, but because **bedbugs couldn't infest brass the way they could wood**. Brass beds also had the advantage—which some savvy manufacturers advertised—of being easier to disassemble and reassemble for regular de-bedbugging of the mattress and linens.

372 ⊱ No solicitors!

Bedbugs probably came to America with the first colonists. Once railroads began to take settlers westward, bedbugs hopped a ride. **Traveling salesmen were particular favorites for bedbugs**, as they went from one cheap hotel to the next and from town to town.

373 ⊱ Coming to a home near you

During the early twentieth century, some surveys found that **one in every three American homes was infested with bedbugs**. The phrase "don't let the bedbugs bite" was no mere idle rhyme.

374 ⊱ It's a chance they were willing to take

Those tormented by bedbugs tried everything to get rid of the tiny pests, including boiling water and smoke. Cyanide fumigation, introduced in the 1920s, did seem to kill the bedbugs—**as well as some homeowners and hotel guests**.

375 ➤ Like a bed of nails, only bouncier

Even though the inner-spring mattress was invented in 1865, it was initially slow to catch on. For one thing, the **springs inside sometimes flipped around so that a sharp, pointy end stuck through into the sleeper's body**. Spring mattresses and box springs didn't really dominate the bedding industry until the 1930s.

376 ➤ We had to fire the servant—he snored

The privacy we take for granted in the bedroom wasn't always so. Having to share a bed was common, and **servants typically slept at the foot of the master's bed**.

377

➤ Talk about a royal flush!

Even in the bathroom, privacy wasn't a given. **Toilets sometimes were made with multiple seats**, so people could do their business simultaneously—and even chat or play cards while they did so.

378 ➤ Flavored water

For convenience, the typical farm well was drilled near the farmhouse—and the barn, pigsty, and chicken coop. **Wastes of all sorts, animal and human, seeped into the household's water supply**.

379 ➤ Incarcerated, but clean
The first place in the United States to enjoy shower baths was not a home but a prison—Eastern State Penitentiary, built in Philadelphia beginning in 1822. The prison also boasted **central heating before the U.S. Capitol had it, and individual flush toilets** long before they were installed at the White House.

380 ➤ The drip, drip, drip of progress
Even in cities, running water remained a rare luxury late into the nineteenth century. In **1882 New York City, only 2 percent of homes were connected to a water system.**

381 ➤ Money down the drain
In the early twentieth century, the cost of a "modern" bathroom—"with all its appurtenances and the perfect care of it, together with the water tax"—was estimated at about **a dollar a day, or 365 dollars per year**. Given that the average salary in 1910 was 750 dollars a year, it's little wonder that many folks stuck with the old-fashioned outhouse and well.

382 ➤ Everything in the kitchen sink
For many families in the early 1900s, **the sole source of water inside the house was the kitchen sink**. There, dishes were washed, teeth brushed, and Saturday-night bathwater was drawn.

383 ➤ The fresh air will do you good
Even being wealthy was no guarantee of owning a serviceable house back when. If you hired an eccentric architect like the celebrated Addison Mizner, for example, you might wind up with the problems faced by client George S. Rasmussen in 1926. Forgetting to include a staircase in his design of the Rasmussens' home, **Mizner made up for his omission by adding an exterior set of stairs**. When it rained, the Rasmussens had to carry an umbrella to go up or downstairs in their expensive home, Casa Nana, in Palm Beach, Florida—where it's been known to rain pretty often.

384 ➤ Get comfortable, you'll be here awhile

Architect Addison Mizner liked to "age" the furniture he used. One such project, however, backfired: Mizner applied quicklime and shellac to make some leather chairs look weatherbeaten. Instead, when people sat down, their body heat caused the shellac to become gooey again—**sticking them and, when the sitters strained to escape, their clothes to the chairs**.

385 ➤ A baah-d idea

The idea of a house having a lawn is relatively recent, because it was very expensive to maintain a stretch of grass before the invention of lawn mowers. One solution adopted by people with large estates was to keep a flock of sheep to "mow" the grass. This technique spread to public spaces as well: **Central Park in New York, for example, maintained a herd of two hundred sheep** and employed a full-time shepherd to tend them.

386 ➤ Not exactly a pony ride

Even after the invention of mechanical lawn mowers, larger lawns relied on horse power—literally—to keep trimmed. "Pony mowers" typically were pulled by a horse with the operator walking behind, and often an apprentice helped guide the horse. The **pony's hooves were often covered by leather boots or slippers to protect the grass**. (There was still, however, the issue of pony poop.) It's said that the Atco Standard, the first successful motorized mower, was invented in 1921 after the pony that had pulled the mower for one of the company's directors died. Instead of investing in a new horse, the director suggested Charles H. Pugh Ltd. try to build a gasoline-powered mower.

387 ➤ You can't break the bonds of blood

In the days before Superglue (introduced in 1958), broken items around the house were stuck back together with whatever was handy. **Early "adhesives" included tar, beeswax, tree sap, egg whites, milk, decomposed animals, even cheese, and blood.** As late as 1940, 95 percent of raw materials in adhesives were still derived from natural sources.

8 NICE WORK IF YOU CAN SURVIVE IT

⤛ Factories, farms and other death traps ⤜

388 ➤ And you thought *your* job was bad!

As cities grew in the nineteenth century, **the profession of "night-soil men" arose to take care of the equally burgeoning problem of human waste,** carting it off to the countryside. Typically working only the late-night shift, between midnight and five in the morning, night-soil men toiled in teams of four. A "hole-man" would climb into the house's cesspit, dislodge the sludge, and shovel it into a tub, which was then hauled up by a "ropeman" and emptied by two "tubmen." On the bright side, night-soil men earned two to three times the wages paid even to skilled workers.

389 ➤ Good thing water porridge goes down quickly

A report on the working conditions of young factory apprentices in 1810 stated that they **labored at their machines from 5:50 in the morning until 9:10 or 9:15 at night**, with two "water porridge" breaks—taken at their machines—and a brief dinner of oatcakes and molasses or oatcakes and "poor broth."

390 ➤ Cracking the whip, literally

In 1828, the radical magazine *The Lion* published an exposé of children's working conditions in factories where the ten-year-old laborers were whipped day and night, not only for the slightest offense but also **to make them work harder, as one might whip a racehorse**.

391 ➤ Lunch break, bring out the pigs!

At another factory exposed by *The Lion*, **child workers were fed slops for which they had to battle the pigs**. The employer also liked to pinch the children's ears until his nails met through the flesh.

392 ➤ Over the hill by age nine

The youngest children made especially good chimney sweeps, as they could wriggle into the tightest and most twisting flues. These **"climbing boys" often began their careers as young as age five**.

393 ➤ Light a fire under them

Employers might "motivate" young chimney sweeps thought to be slacking off by **setting fire to a pile of straw in the hearth below the sweeps**.

394 ➤ Cruelty, A to Z

A campaigner for child-labor reform recalled visiting a textile factory in 1838 and observing a sampling of eighty child workers who had become crippled and deformed on the job: "No power of language could describe the varieties, and I may say the cruelties, in all these degradations of the human form. **They stood or squatted before me in all the shapes of the letters of the alphabet.** This was the effect of prolonged toil on the tender frames of children at early ages."

395 ➤ School daze

Child labor typically meant no schooling for young workers. In 1836, Massachusetts was the first state to mandate that children working in factories had to attend school—**all of three months a year**.

396 ➤ Hi Mom, I'm home early!

Children worked from dawn until dusk with no legal limits until 1842, when Massachusetts again struck a blow for "reform"—**limiting children to working no more than ten hours a day**.

397 ➤ Generous to a fault

The parents of child laborers who were crippled in industrial accidents typically got **as little as one dollar in compensation from the employer**. To collect even that pittance, they had to sign away any right to sue.

398 ➤ Giving the young-uns a head start

In the late 1800s, one in three mill workers in the United States was a child. Overall, **more than 1.7 million children were working as of 1900**, and in southern states, the share of child laborers actually tripled from 1890 to 1900.

399 ➤ Not exactly kids' stuff

Child labor peaked in the United States in the early decades of the twentieth century, with children working everywhere from mines, canneries, and textile factories to jobs as newsboys, bootblacks, and peddlers. From the employer's standpoint, **children were the ideal workers**: small enough to crawl under machinery and into tight mine shafts, paid less than adults, and easily bullied by "strappers" working as enforcers for the boss.

400 ➤ Putting a lot of eight-year-olds out of work

Minimum ages of employment and **hours of work for children were not regulated by federal law until 1938,** with the passage of the Fair Labor Standards Act.

401 ➤ A stitch in time, or else

Women weavers in the 1830s earned 1.25 to two dollars a week while working sixteen to seventeen hours a day—and **could be fired for being even a few minutes late to work.** They had to buy their own needles and thread from the owner.

402 ➤ The thirteen-hour workday

Factory work in the late 1870s was described by one reform advocate: "**a continuity of toil, in a standing position, in a poisonous atmosphere,** during thirteen hours, with fifteen minutes of rest."

403 ➤ Plus all the coal dust you can eat

In the late 1800s, company stores depleted the already poor wages of many workers, who were **paid in "scrip" that was worthless elsewhere.** Pennsylvania coal-mining families, for example, paid nearly a third more for butter and two dollars a barrel more for flour at the company store.

404 ➤ Truly driven

In the early 1880s, streetcar drivers in New York City **earned a paltry twelve dollars a day while working sixteen hours daily**. When they demanded a reduction to a twelve-hour workday, then-State Assemblyman Theodore Roosevelt called the idea "communistic."

405 ➤ That's shoe biz

Efforts to unionize—**by 1900 fewer than one worker in thirty belonged to a labor union**—were dealt with swiftly, with the stroke of a pen if not a hired goon's billy club. One New England shoe manufacturer fired all his employees and replaced them with Chinese workers brought in from the West Coast who would do the same work for just twenty-six dollars a week.

406 ➤ Help wanted, bring your own gun

Railroad developer and speculator Jay Gould had his own solution to labor problems: "**I can hire one half of the working class to kill the other half.**"

407 ➤ No timecards needed

Annual hours of work actually rose by about 10 percent for most laborers in the nineteenth century, despite increased mechanization. The only laborers whose work hours went down were former slaves, whose average per capita labor hours fell 26 to 35 percent.

408 ➤ Every rose has its thorns

Factories that made silk flowers applied plenty of arsenic in compounds that produced bright colors in their products. Unfortunately for the workers making the flowers, exposure to **arsenic also caused nausea, sores, and swelling of the arms and legs, often leading to complete disability**.

409 ➤ Working their fingers to the bone
Workers in soap-making factories were routinely exposed to caustic chemicals that turned their fingernails yellow and even began to **eat away at their fingers**.

410 ➤ No exit
When fire broke out at the Triangle Shirtwaist Company factory in New York City in 1911, **many of the garment workers were trapped because managers had locked the stairwell and exit doors**. Those who didn't die by jumping from as high as the tenth floor perished from fire and smoke inhalation—146 in all, mostly immigrant women, ranging in age from forty-eight to fourteen.

411 ➤ Idle hands not a problem here
In the wake of the 1911 Triangle Shirtwaist fire, some of the garment workers who survived talked about their working conditions. In peak season, **work hours ran from 7:30 in the morning until nine at night**.

412 ➤ The seventy-seven-hour workweek
The "mill girls" employed at textile factories typically **worked twelve to fourteen hours a day, Monday through Friday, with half a day on Saturday** and Sundays off. Reformers, such as Sarah Bagley, campaigned for a ten-hour workday. Bagley wrote that she represented those "who are not willing to see our sex made into living machines."

413 ➤ The style is cramped—at home and work

Fresh off the farm, "mill girls" slept **two to a bed, four to a room, in crowded boardinghouses.** What scant free time they had was closely monitored by overseers, who enforced strict curfews and codes of conduct in the women's boardinghouses.

414 ➤ Seven dwarves, you're outta here!

Workers in some factories could be **fired simply for looking out the window or whistling** while they worked.

415 ➤ And no 401(k), either

In the nineteenth century, a **live-in maid might earn less than $35 a year**, while a general servant might make as much as $90 annually. Better paid, butlers could earn about $230 a year.

416 ➤ The early bird gets the shoe polish

Household servants put in long hours doing punishing work, too. One retired servant, writing in 1925, recalled how his typical day began with **polishing twenty pairs of boots, tending to more than thirty lamps and getting a fire going**—all before his employer's family even got out of bed.

417 ➤ When did bathing become in vogue?

When members of the household desired a bath, a servant would have to **carry some 350 pounds of hot water upstairs.** Multiply that by the number of people in the family, plus any guests.

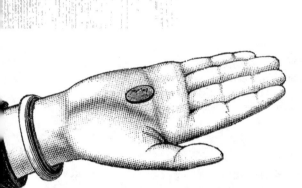

418 ➤ Finder's keepers does not apply

Household servants faced the constant risk of being "let go" and had good reason to be paranoid: Many employers would **"test" their servants' honesty by leaving some valuable or a spare coin in plain sight**, to see if the underpaid servant could be tempted to pocket it.

419 ➤ Summon What's-his-name to clean this up!

Even servants' own names were subject to the whims of their employers. Rather than bother to learn a new servant's name—after, perhaps, his or her predecessor had been let go or moved on to less-onerous service—**the head of a household might simply call the servant by the predecessor's name**. So, for example, one butler after another might be summoned as "Jeeves," regardless of the butler's actual name.

420 ➤ At least we know the stuff works

Long hours and hard work weren't the only woes for some workers in the good old days, who perished in one horrific industrial accident after another. Perhaps not surprisingly, among the notable workplace explosions was the 1918 blowup of a Pennsylvania plant that manufactured TNT. **The Aetna Chemical Company blast killed some two hundred people**.

421 ➤ Maybe blow torches were a bad idea

In November 1927, twenty-eight people were killed and five hundred injured when the world's largest natural-gas tank—a seventy-five-foot-tall structure in Pittsburgh—**exploded while workers attempted to make repairs using blow torches**. (They thought the tank was empty at the time.) The explosion rocketed the tank into the air in a ball of fire, then set off two neighboring gas tanks. Chunks of metal flew more than a mile in the air. In the city, shattered glass from skyscraper windows rained down on pedestrians and streets buckled, bursting water mains and flooding some areas waist-deep.

422 ➤ Lowering the boom

The worst industrial accident in the United States occurred in 1947, when an explosion of fertilizer cargo aboard the *Grandcamp*, docked in the Texas City, Texas, harbor, **killed nearly 600 dockworkers and Monsanto Chemical Company employees**. Another 3,500 people suffered injuries from the blast, which tossed chunks of steel a mile and shattered windows twenty-five miles away.

423 ➤ Fire and ice

The Chicago Crib Disaster of 1909 was one of the worst ever to strike the construction industry: When fire broke out on a temporary water crib, part of a water project for the city of Chicago, **it quickly reached the dynamite storehouse and a dormitory** that housed the construction workers. About sixty workers died—the total is uncertain because many were burned beyond recognition and others' bodies were never recovered. A few survived the January blast by crawling out onto ice floes on Lake Michigan, only to drown or freeze to death.

424

➤ Digging their own graves

The worst coal-mine disaster in United States history occurred in Monongah, West Virginia, in 1907, when an explosion killed at least 362 men and boys working in the mine. Unofficial reports put the death toll as high as five hundred. That year alone—prior to establishment of the U.S. Bureau of Mines, which helped improve mine safety—**coal-mining accidents and explosions claimed 2,534 lives in the United States**.

425 ➤ **One group not longing for yesteryear**

Today, coal mining remains among the most dangerous occupations, with about nine deaths a year for every 100,000 miners. But back in 1900, that rate was **three hundred deaths for every 100,000 coal miners**.

426 ➤ Ol' King Coal

A 1962 coal-mine fire in Centralia, Pennsylvania, eventually forced the evacuation of the town; once home to one thousand people, Centralia now has only ten residents. One observer described the fire as seen up close: "This was a world where no human could live, hotter than the planet Mercury, its atmosphere as poisonous as Saturn's. At the heart of the fire, temperatures easily exceeded 1,000 degrees [Fahrenheit]. Lethal clouds of carbon monoxide and other gases swirled through the rock chambers." **The coal-mine fire continues to burn a half-century later**, as it may continue to do for another 250 years.

427 ➤ Flour power

Who would think that grain dust could explode? In 1878, the Washburn "A" Mill in Minneapolis blew up when **dust from grain, destined to make flour, ignited**. The blast killed eighteen mill workers and destroyed a third of Minneapolis' milling capacity.

428 ➤ Plenty of opportunity for promotion

The first systematic survey of workplace fatalities in the twentieth-century United States studied Ardmore County, Pennsylvania. **In just one twelve-month stretch in 1906 and 1907, in that single county, 526 workers were killed on the job.**

429 ➤ Dying to work here

In a nationwide tally of workplace fatalities in 1913, the Bureau of Labor Statistics documented 23,000 on-the-job deaths. Given a workforce at the time of approximately 38 million, that comes out to a whopping **sixty-one deaths a year per 100,000 laborers.**

430 ➤ So sue me!

Workers killed or injured on the job had an uphill battle to get any compensation from their employers. If the boss could show that a worker was partly at fault or had knowingly assumed the risk, or could blame another employee, courts typically awarded nothing in workplace negligence claims. Even if a judgment did go against the company, **the average compensation for a fatal injury in 1900 was just six months' pay.**

9

NO WONDER THEY CALL IT THE "DISMAL SCIENCE"

⤖ Money and economics, the rich and (mostly) the poor ⤖

431 ➤ Don't tell the IRS about this!

After the Vikings invaded Ireland, beginning in 795, they introduced coins—and taxes—to the Emerald Isle. In ninth century Ireland, **those who refused to pay the Vikings' "tax" got their noses slit**, which is the origin of the phrase "pay through the nose."

432 ➤ And a happy new year!

Debasement of the currency by reducing its precious-metal content was a constant problem in the Middle Ages, although some rulers encouraged it as a source of easy money. Not so England's King Henry I, who **punished the nation's mint masters at the Assize of Winchester on Christmas Day in 1124 by cutting off their right hands**.

433 ➤ Who decided the menu for the investors' lunch?

Tulip mania swept Dutch investors in the seventeenth century. But the aftermath, when prices crashed in the 1670s, is even more, er, colorful: A mob of angry investors attacked and **killed the prime minister, then—according to some accounts—partially ate him**.

434 ➤ The first greenback?

Short on official British money, the Virginia colony resorted to **using tobacco leaves as currency**. When this grew too inconvenient, in 1727 "tobacco notes" certifying the quality and quantity of tobacco held in warehouses became legal tender.

435 ➤ Hot under the collar about taxes?

"Tally sticks," hazelwood sticks notched and then split so both parties had matching halves, were used to keep track of tax collections in England until 1826. The obsolete sticks were then stored in the Palace of Westminster, home to Parliament—until 1834, when **they were burned in the furnace that heated the House of Lords**. Workmen over stoked the furnace, then left for the night. By morning, the blaze had destroyed both Houses of Parliament.

436 ➤ Maybe Britain would take us back?

The first financial panic to strike the new United States, post-independence, was the "Panic of 1792." Speculators caused a run on the Bank of New York, and **securities lost 25 percent of their value in just two weeks**, until Secretary of the Treasury Alexander Hamilton succeeded in stabilizing markets by propping up the troubled bank.

437 ➤ Time to panic, again

The "Panic of 1837" saw 250 financial enterprises close in New York City alone during the first three weeks of April. **Eight states soon found themselves wholly or partially unable to pay their debts**. Nationwide, 343 of a total of 850 banks closed their doors, a shock from which the system of state banks never recovered.

438 ➤ War is an expensive business

The Civil War cost the United States roughly $6.7 billion. In today's money, however, that would be the equivalent of $139 billion. If all the costs of the war's economic disruption were totaled up, **the true cost of the Civil War would come to about $46 trillion in today's dollars.**

439 ➤ It takes two to tangle the economy

Before there was Black Tuesday in 1929 (and the other "black" days of that crash), there was Black Friday—September 29, 1869. Unlike most "panics" that took down the U.S. economy, Black Friday was mostly **caused by just two men**, speculators James Fisk and Jay Gould. Their efforts to corner the gold market led to a 30 percent rise in gold prices, followed by plummeting prices when the federal government stepped in and sold some of its own gold holdings. Many investors lost fortunes, but Fisk and Gould got out in time.

440 ➤ People who know people

A Congressional investigation of the Black Friday panic of 1869 helped reveal that speculators James Fisk and Jay Gould had used financier Abel Corbin, a brother-in-law of President Ulysses S. Grant, to get close to the president and argue against government sales of gold, which would bring the price down and devalue their holdings. Corbin also got his presidential brother-in-law to appoint General Daniel Butterfield as assistant treasurer of the United States; in return, **Butterfield agreed to tip off the speculators if the treasury planned any gold sales**. When the gold balloon ultimately collapsed, Corbin was financially ruined.

441 ➤ Another reason to panic

The closing of Jay Cooke & Company, a large and respected bank that had helped the federal government finance the Civil War and underwrote the construction of the Northern Pacific Railroad, triggered the "Panic of 1873." Investors in Europe, which was already suffering its own economic woes, began calling in their loans to American companies. As the panic swept Wall Street, **the New York Stock Exchange closed its doors for ten days**.

442

➤ A bitter harvest

"Losing the farm" was a real concern in the economic downturn of the 1880s. Nearly 40 percent of American farmers became tenants on what had, in most cases, formerly been their own land. **Many mortgaged their farms to the railroads**, who were quick to foreclose and make farmers homeless.

443 ➤ The sun'll come out tomorrow?

In the 1880s, **an estimated 100,000 homeless children roamed the streets of New York City**. So pitiful was their condition that when one social worker was unable to find help for a little girl she'd rescued, the do-gooder appealed to the Society for the Prevention of Cruelty to Animals. Reasoning that the child was indeed an animal, the society agreed to lend a hand.

444 ➤ The 1 percent

The rising economic tide of the Gilded Age didn't exactly lift all boats. By 1890, **the richest 1 percent of Americans possessed more wealth than the poorest 99 percent combined**.

445 ➤ Let's hope they got employee discounts

The department-store magnate Marshall Field earned as much in an hour as the shop girls who worked for him made in three to four years. While Field's employees were paid three to five dollars a week, it was estimated that **Field himself was paid the equivalent of six hundred dollars an hour**.

446 ➤ Enough rope to hang themselves

Until the Great Depression, the "Panic of 1893" was the United States' most severe financial crisis. **More than five hundred banks failed and fifteen thousand businesses closed their doors**. Among the triggers for the panic was the financial distress of the National Cordage Company, a maker of rope that was the stock market's most actively traded company. The company had tried to corner the market for imported hemp, used in rope making, and wound up going bankrupt instead.

447 ➤ Buddy, can you spare $65 million?

So dire was the Panic of 1893, which led to a run on the United States' gold reserves that backed the dollar, that **President Grover Cleveland had to borrow $65 million in gold from the wealthy J.P. Morgan** to prop up the nation's currency.

448 ➤ A nation with prices on the rise

The worst period of inflation in American history came right at the nation's beginning, during the American Revolution, when **costs rose at an annual rate of about 23 percent.** During the Civil War, inflation reached about 20 percent.

449 ➤ Talk about shelling out

Not only Western nations suffered runaway inflation. In Uganda, cowry shells were first used as currency about 1800, when two shells were enough to purchase a woman. Unchecked importation of the shells caused prices to soar, however, and **by 1860 the price of a woman had risen to one thousand cowries**.

450 ➤ Prices are subject to immediate change

At the peak of Germany's hyperinflation in 1923, a wheelbarrow full of money wasn't enough to buy a newspaper and **few bothered to collect the change when they spent the new 1,000-billion mark note**. One student at Freiburg University ordered a cup of coffee, priced on the menu at five thousand marks, then a second. When the bill came, it was for fourteen thousand marks; the price had jumped in-between cups. "If you want to save money," he was told, "you should order them both at the same time."

451 ➤ How good is your multiplication?

Even America's worst bouts with inflation were nothing compared to post-World War II Hungary. Setting a record for the most rapid monthly hyperinflation, in July 1946 **prices doubled every thirteen and a half hours—an annual rate of 41.9 quadrillion percent.**

452 ➤ You're going to need a bigger wallet

If you wanted to do business among the Kirghiz people of central Asia, as recently as 1910, you needed horses, which were the main form of currency. Sheep were used as subsidiary units of money, and **change was given in lambskins.**

453 ➤ Caution, falling stockbrokers ahead

Recent financial gyrations make it easy to dismiss the 1929 stock market crash as just another bear market. But the selling frenzy of "Black Tuesday," October 29, 1929, the single worst day of the stock market crash, **wiped out $15 billion in assets—the equivalent of $190 billion today.** Humorist Will Rogers cracked, "You had to stand in line to get a window to jump out of, and speculators were selling space for bodies in the East River."

454 ➤ Sometimes the bear market eats you

Over the span of a "black" week in 1929, Wall Street suffered losses totaling $30 billion—the equivalent of $380 billion today. **The stock-market losses totaled more than the United States had spent in all of World War I** and more than the annual federal budget.

455 ➤ Why investors need patience, and lots of it

The Dow Jones Industrial Average, which had reached a peak of 381 points less than two months before Black Tuesday in 1929, dropped 89 percent before finally hitting bottom at 42 points in 1932. **The stock-market index would not recover to its September 3, 1929, level until 1955**—twenty-six years later.

456 ➤ And how long will you be staying with us?

So many ruined financiers committed suicide in the wake of the 1929 stock market crash that clerks at one Wall Street hotel were said to **ask guests as they checked in whether they needed the room for sleeping or for jumping.**

457 ➤ Breathe deep and your troubles will disappear

Asphyxiation by gas was actually the most popular way to end it all after the 1929 crash, according to historian William K. Klingaman, though the financially ruined were nothing if not inventive: "The wife of a Long Island broker shot herself in the heart; a utilities executive in Rochester, New York, shut himself in his bathroom and opened a wall jet of illuminating gas; a St. Louis broker swallowed poison; a Philadelphia financier shot himself in his athletic club; a divorcee in Allentown, Pennsylvania, closed the doors and windows of her home and turned on a gas oven. In Milwaukee, one gentleman who took his own life left a note that read, **"My body should go to science, my soul to Andrew W. Mellon, and sympathy to my creditors."**

458 ➤ Banker's hours are about to get even shorter

Bank failures were among the frightening hallmarks of the Great Depression. By 1933, **11,000 of the United States' 25,000 banks had shut their doors**. Before the creation of the Federal Deposit Insurance Corporation (FDIC), when banks failed, their depositors often lost everything they had. By 1933, depositors in failed banks had lost assets totaling $140 billion.

459 ➤ Not the kind of increase you want to see

In the decade before the Depression, only about seventy banks failed a year across the entire United States. In just the first ten months of 1930, however, 744 banks failed—**more than during the previous ten years combined**.

460 ➤ But the pink-slip business was booming

At the depths of the Great Depression in 1933, unemployment reached 25 percent—and 37 percent of non-farm employment. Another 25 percent of people who still had jobs took wage cuts or saw their hours shaved to part-time. Some places were especially hard hit by unemployment: Half of all workers in Cleveland, Ohio, were jobless, and in **Toledo, Ohio, unemployment reached 80 percent**. Nationally, not until 1941 did unemployment fall back below the 10 percent mark.

461 ➤ Half the product it used to be

The Great Depression saw the United States' gross national product, the total of the nation's goods and services produced, **fall by almost 50 percent**.

462 ➤ Not the legacy Herb was hoping for

"Hoovervilles," derisively named for President Herbert Hoover, whose economic policies were partly blamed for the Depression, sprang up across the country as homeless Americans found shelter in tents, packing crates, and abandoned vehicles. Besides "Hoovervilles," the scorned president was remembered in **"Hoover blankets"** (newspapers under which the homeless huddled), "Hoover wagons" (broken-down automobiles that were pulled by mules), "Hoover stew" (the fare served in soup kitchens), and "Hoover hogs" (jackrabbits caught and eaten in lieu of pork).

463 ➤ That will stunt your growth

Roughly half of American children **lacked adequate food, shelter, or medical care** during the depths of the Great Depression.

464 ➤ Something to be depressed about

The Great Depression was compounded by the Dust Bowl years in America's heartland. Drought and over farming combined with the economic downturn to make **a million acres of farmland worthless**.

465 ➤ Silence of the lambs

Weak prices for their products during the Depression also contributed to the plight of America's farmers. According to one story, a sheep farmer who realized that he couldn't afford to keep feeding his flock and wouldn't make enough from selling them or their wool, decided instead to **slit the throats of all three thousand starving sheep and toss their bodies into a canyon**.

466 ➤ Old McDonald lost a farm…

Between 1930 and 1935, **almost 750,000 U.S. farms were lost to bankruptcy** or foreclosure sales.

467 ➤ How low can you go?

Some farmers who despaired of keeping their farms out of the hands of creditors in the Depression resorted to colluding with sympathetic neighbors in "Penny Auctions." The crowd would keep the bidding for a bankrupt farm down to a few pennies, so the farmer could afford to buy back the property. Anyone who tried to bid higher quickly got the message, sometimes by farmers who **dangled nooses at bidders who didn't go along with the scheme**.

468 ➤ The thanks of a grateful nation

Veterans of World War I were also hit hard by the Depression. Their plight led to the "bonus army" march on Washington, D.C., in 1932, which demanded that the federal government pay immediately the veterans' bonuses **scheduled to be paid in 1945**. The U.S. Army was finally called out to disperse the "bonus army."

469 ➤ Share this fact with ten friends

One of the ways hard-pressed Americans tried to make a buck during the Depression was the chain letter, which originated in the mid-1930s as a get-rich-quick scheme. Despite the fact they failed to make anybody rich, **chain letters became so popular that post offices had to hire extra help to handle the volume of mail**—virtually the only place during the Depression that did any hiring.

10 LOW SOCIETY

Fads, fallacies, and fancies, holidays, and living high on the hog

470 ➤ I'll jump right behind you!

Predicting the end of the world has long been a popular way to gain attention—though it seldom ends well. Way back in 448, Moses of Crete, a rabbi, claimed to be the Messiah as predicted by Talmudic calculations and led his followers to the sea, which was supposed to part so they could reach Palestine. Having given away all their possessions, the **rabbi's followers cast themselves into the Mediterranean**. Seeing them crash on the rocks or drown, the rabbi declined to follow and "suddenly disappeared," leading some to conclude he had actually been "some malignant fiend" in human form.

471 ➤ Noah made it seem so easy...

Then there were the astrological predictions that a 1524 planetary alignment in Pisces would produce an apocalypse. People in Germany built boats, including **a three-story ark** constructed by a Count von Iggleheim, and residents of port cities took refuge afloat. When doomsday arrived with only a light drizzle, angry crowds outside the ark stampeded, trampling hundreds, and stoned the count to death.

472 ➤ Which came first, the message or the egg?

The fad for fortune-telling took many forms. In 1809, fortune-teller Mary Bateman produced eggs with apocalyptic messages on them she claimed were **laid by a magic chicken**. She was later caught "priming" the chicken with a prepared egg and subsequently hanged for poisoning a client.

473 ➤ Mark your calendar!

In America, forerunners of today's Seventh-day Adventists, the Millerites, followed Baptist preacher William Miller, who concluded Christ would return in 1844. Another Millerite pegged it more precisely as October 22, 1844, a day that came to be known as "the Great Disappointment." **Thousands of followers gave away their possessions and awaited the end.** When Jesus didn't appear, one wrote, "I lay prostrate for two days without any pain—sick with disappointment." Even children in the streets would taunt the disappointed Millerites, "Have you not gone up [to heaven]?"

474 ➤ Put that in your pipe and smoke it

Soon after tobacco was discovered in the New World, **smoking was thought to be a cure-all and even to sweeten bad breath.** One early smoker's wife, however, disagreed, telling her husband, "It makes your breath stink like the piss of a fox."

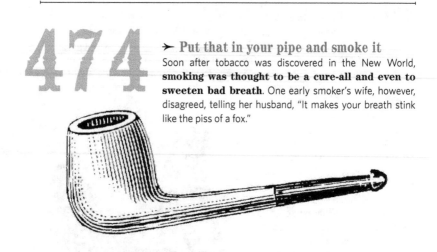

475 ➤ And you thought discarded butts were bad

To make smoking more convenient, tobacco vendors offered **pre-filled, disposable pipes.** The used pipes would then be thrown away, typically into the nearest river.

476

➤ Looks like you have a sweet tooth

In the eighteenth century, sugar was so popular, despite its high price, that people whose teeth had not yet blackened from decay **artificially colored their teeth black** to show that they were wealthy enough to splurge on sugar.

477 ➤ He saved face—but lost his life

An excess of etiquette can be fatal. Danish astronomer Tycho Brahe supposedly died in 1601 of a bladder or kidney ailment contracted at a banquet in Prague when he "**refused to leave the banquet to relieve himself** because it would have been a breach of etiquette."

478 ➤ Money doesn't equal manners

Not everyone got the niceties of etiquette—not even the richest Americans. Fur baron John Jacob Astor once astonished guests at a fancy dinner party by **wiping his hands using the dress of the lady seated next to him.**

479 ➤ Really, that's just going too far

A popular American etiquette handbook advised readers that they "may wipe their lips on the table cloth, but **not blow their noses with it**."

480 ➤ Your stomach will let you know later

Another guide to manners cautioned members of polite society that it was considered impolite to **sniff a piece of meat on one's fork to make sure it had not gone bad**.

481 ➤ One is the loneliest number

In the 1700s, people who had nothing better to do with their money indulged in a fad for hermits. Wealthy landowners would build a hermitage on their estates and then **hire a live-in hermit to occupy the crude dwelling**. Some live-in hermits were required to take monk-like vows of silence as part of their employment. Not everyone could cut it as a hermit, however, and those who were caught sneaking out to throw back a few drinks in the local pub would be summarily dismissed.

482 ➤ Bah, humbug!

Until 1681 in New England, **people who had a good time on Christmas could be fined five shillings**. The Puritans and others considered secular celebrations of Christmas as "wanton Bacchanalian Feasts," and declared December 25 instead a day of fasting and penance. Any celebrating, including feasting or just taking the day off from work, earned a fine.

483 ➤ Redcoat and green

Christmas celebrating took another blow with the American Revolution, because the hated British tended to make a bigger spectacle of yuletime. **American patriots came to link Christmas with Tories and Loyalists.**

484 ➤ Seasons Greetings?

Christmas cards have long had a secular bent, depicting holly, mistletoe, and plum pudding from the very beginning. But some nineteenth-century Christmas cards took this to an extreme with **bizarre and even vulgar scenes of scantily clad girls, devils, bugs, and rats.**

485 ⤳ An X-rated Xmas tradition

Victorians adopted the mistletoe from the ancient Roman mistletoe tradition of the Saturnalia. The Christmas custom of "**kissing under the mistletoe**" is a toned-down version of the sexual license of the Roman holiday.

486 ⤳ Santa Gnome

Before illustrator Thomas Nast gave Saint Nicholas a visual upgrade in the pages of *Harper's Weekly*, from 1862 through 1886, **not-so-jolly old Saint Nick was variously depicted as a frock-clad gnome** and a stern-faced bishop.

487 ⤳ No treats, no trickery

Halloween also had a hard time gaining acceptance as a holiday. **The Puritan ethos of colonial New England discouraged celebrations of Halloween**, which originally took hold as a harvest festival in the southern states.

488 ➤ We could be carving carrots instead of pumpkins

Halloween caught on in America after the 1846 potato famine with the arrival of Irish immigrants, who brought the jack o'lantern with them. The **original jack o'lantern tale, however, is pretty grisly**: Jack trapped the devil in a tree until the devil agreed that Jack, a notorious sinner, wouldn't go to hell when he died. The devil gave Jack a burning ember from hell to light his way through the dark places of the earth, since heaven was forbidden to him, and Jack placed it in a lantern made of a carrot or turnip. Placing the "burning ember from hell" in pumpkins proved more practical after the Irish got to America.

489 ➤ Conjuring Mr. Right

For young women, Halloween was "San-Apple Night," when it was believed that **girls could predict the name or appearance of their future husbands** by Halloween magic with mirrors, yarn, or apple parings or by bobbing for apples.

490 ➤ Sugar's probably not the best way to calm them

Some popular histories of Halloween maintain that "trick or treating" was popularized by adults as a way to **bribe youngsters not to commit acts of vandalism**. For example, Ze Jumbo Jelly Beans were packaged with the message, "Stop Halloween Pranksters."

491 ⟩ Why are you at my door dressed like that?

As late as the 1950s, **some adults viewed trick or treating as a form of extortion**—or had to have the Halloween traditions explained to them by the costumed children at their door.

492 ⟩ Hi yo, silverware!

The opulence of the "Gilded Age" led to some jaw-dropping extremes. One lavish New York dinner party took over the ballroom of the posh Sherry's restaurant for a Wild West theme: Dinner guests, dressed in cowboy attire, **ate on horseback**—a peculiar indulgence made possible by leading several dozen horses into the restaurant, hooves padded to protect the floors, and tethering the mounts to tables.

493 ⟩ Someone has blown a fuse...

At another extravagant affair, thrown by Mrs. William K. Vanderbilt in 1883, **the hostess came dressed as an electric light**. More illuminating was the fact that the party cost $250,000—nearly $5.8 million in today's dollars.

494 ⟩ This is why the rich have chauffeurs

Another Vanderbilt, Cornelius's son Reggie, was so rich he literally got away with murder. An infamously reckless motorist, Reggie was involved with five separate pedestrian accidents in New York City, **killing two victims and crippling another**. Yet young Vanderbilt was never charged with so much as reckless driving.

495 ➤ Shoot another one, darling, I need a hatbox!

But the prize for conspicuous consumption has to go to Mrs. Edward T. Stotesbury, doyenne of El Mirasol estate in Florida (as well as the 147-room Whitemarsh Hall outside Philadelphia and Wingwood in Bar Harbor, Maine). "Queen Eva," as she was called, once spent **half a million dollars on a hunting trip with friends just to kill alligators sufficient to cover a set of suitcases.**

496 ➤ So much for birthday cake...

How uptight were the Victorians? It was **considered shocking for a woman to blow out candles in mixed company**, because to do so required pursing her lips in a manner that might be seen as suggestive.

497 ➤ Nudge-nudge, wink-wink, know what I mean?

Women in Victorian times were also **forbidden to say they were "going to bed,"** lest someone within hearing put an erotic interpretation on that phrase. Instead, a proper lady would say, "I am going to retire for the night."

498 ➤ When Hugh Hefner was a tyke

The slang of the 1920s says a lot about the status of women in that day. Girls or women were "broads," "bunnies," "dames," and "dolls." A woman who could sing was a "canary." **One who was sexually promiscuous was a "charity girl."**

499 ➤ If you can't beat them, domesticate them!

Rats became fashionable companions in the nineteenth century, when you might see **a lady out for a stroll with a beribboned rat on a leash.** Pet rats soon invaded shows held by mouse fanciers, and for a time in the early 1900s, England's National Mouse Club was renamed the National Mouse and Rat Club.

500

➤ The spirits say, "Yes!"

The Ouija board, an otherworldly fad in the 1920s when people believed it could connect them to the spirit world, was invented by Charles Kennard. He claimed the word "Ouija" had been **dictated to him from beyond** by the moving planchette on the board, and that it was an ancient Egyptian word meaning "good luck." When an employee of Kennard's, William Fuld, took over the Ouija business, he switched to a more plausible etymology: "Ouija" came from combining the word for "yes" in French ("oui") and German ("ja").

501 ➤ Old MacDonald had an ant...

The ant farm—more grandly called a "formicarium"—was patented in 1931 by Dartmouth engineering professor Frank Austin. The most popular brand, "Uncle Milton's Ant Farm," depicted whimsical "farm" scenes, below which ants would labor to build their tunnels; **purchasers would mail in a coupon included with the ant farm to receive a shipment of live ants**. Although various substances, including vegetable oil and petroleum jelly, were used to prevent ants from escaping a formicarium, breakouts were still possible. Owners weary of seeing escaped ants crawling about their living rooms sometimes resorted to using multiple techniques, including surrounding the entire formicarium in a "moat" of vegetable oil.

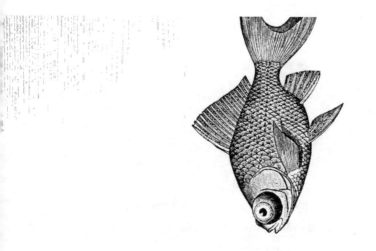

502 ➤ The catch of the day

Yes, people really did swallow goldfish. The fad started in 1938 when Harvard freshman Lothrop Withington Jr. **downed a live goldfish**, followed by a mashed-potato chaser.

503 ➤ Khrushchev probably just couldn't make it spin

The all-time standard for fads was set by the hula-hoop, introduced by Wham-O in 1958 at the price of $1.98. Within two years, 100 million were sold worldwide and Wham-O was manufacturing 20,000 a day; the plastic tubing used to make all the hula-hoops ever manufactured would stretch around Earth five times. But not everyone loved the craze: **Japan banned the hoops because of the "suggestive" motion required to spin them**, and the USSR condemned them as emblematic of the "emptiness of American culture."

504 ➤ They weren't using it, anyway

Did 1940s scrap drives really help the war effort? Historians now say the packrat-ing of everything from scrap paper to tinfoil from gum wrappers did more for home front morale than for military material. And sometimes scrap drives went too far, as when **a historic Civil War cannon from Fort Omaha was melted down**.

505 ➤ Mr. Kilroy, it's a girl!

World War II soldiers liked to mark where they'd been with a stylized drawing of a nose and eyes and the words, "Kilroy was here." The slogan remained popular after the troops came home, and **pregnant women were seen in the delivery room with "Kilroy was here"** painted on their bellies.

506 ➤ Monkey sea, monkey die

"Sea Monkeys"—originally called **"Instant Life"** by inventor Harold von Braunhut—were actually simply brine shrimp, tiny crustaceans with short lifespans. Children who ordered Sea Monkeys based on omnipresent ads in comic books depicting creatures with an almost humanoid appearance were disappointed when the Sea Monkeys turned out to be nothing like the pictures—and then the brine shrimp died.

507 ➤ If it had been winter, the bet would have been double

"Streaking" actually dates to at least July 1799, when a British man was arrested after he'd accepted a **ten-guinea bet to run naked from Cornhill to Cheapside**.

508

➤ Maybe voters liked what they saw...

The first streaking incident on a U.S. college campus may have occurred in 1804, when Washington College senior George William Crump was arrested for running naked through the college town of Lexington, Virginia. The arrest got Crump suspended, but didn't hurt his future prospects, as **he was later elected to Congress.**

509 ➤ It's an official part of the college experience

After the Civil War, as president of Washington College (now Washington and Lee University), former Confederate general **Robert E. Lee officially approved streaking as a rite of passage** for students at the school.

510 ➤ Letting it all hang out

Streaking returned to college campuses as a fad in the 1960s and especially the early 1970s. The use of the term "streaking" to mean running naked dates to 1973, and was popularized by a reporter covering (or uncovering) **a mass nude run by 533 University of Maryland students**.

511 ➤ What's the color for feeling ripped off?

Mood rings, a fad in the 1970s, supposedly reflected the wearer's emotional state by measuring small fluctuations in a person's body temperature caused by mood changes. The tiny temperature changes would cause a liquid crystal in the ring to turn different colors. Actually, however, **changes in the ambient air temperature had a greater effect on the "mood ring" than the wearer's emotions**; no association between the person's mood and the mood ring's color was ever really proven.

512 ➤ For the person who has rocks in his head

Another 1970s fad, Pet Rocks, was introduced by advertising executive Gary Dahl at a gift show in 1975. Sold for $3.95 each, the rocks were packaged with an owner's manual in a box designed to look like a pet carrying case. **More than a million Pet Rocks were sold**, and three tons of stone from Rosarita Beach in Baja, Mexico, were excavated to supply the demand.

11 WE ARE NOT AMUSED

Sports, recreation, and what
our ancestors called "fun"

513 ➤ This week on "The Roman Sportsman"

Animal combat was a popular sport in ancient Rome. Special scenery was even constructed for the *venatio*, **a staged hunt that took place through transplanted trees, man-made hills, and even artificial lakes**. Inevitably, the hunts ended in the animals' deaths, but often some hunters perished as well.

514 ➤ The original crocodile hunters

The Romans' appetite for exotic animals for sporting entertainment was so high that **the army had a special position, *venator immunis*, for soldiers who procured animals.** As audiences became inured to ordinary species, the animals became ever more exotic: lions and panthers in 186 B.C., bears and elephants in 169 B.C., crocodiles and hippos in 58 B.C. During the inaugural games of the Colosseum in Rome in 80 A.D., between 3,500 and 9,000 animals were killed.

515 ➤ Rome wasn't built in a day, but this stadium was...

As though gladiatorial combat weren't grisly enough, sometimes spectators in Roman amphitheaters perished as well—by the thousands. One notable sports disaster occurred in 27 A.D., when fifty thousand fans jammed into a newly built stadium in suburban Fidenae. Little did they know that the builder had cut corners on the foundation supporting the tens of thousands of seats: As the weight of arriving spectators grew, the stadium creaked, teetered, and finally collapsed in a chaos of broken timbers, bodies and screams. **Estimates of the dead and injured at Fidenae range from twenty thousand on up**.

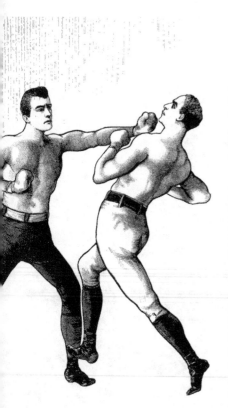

516 ➤ Really down for the count

Early boxing had no referees, no weight divisions, and no limits on the number of rounds. Jack Broughton introduced the first rules in 1743 **in hopes of reducing the number of boxers who died in the ring**.

517 ➤ Mike Tyson didn't get the memo about biting

Prior to the "Prize Ring Rules," enacted in 1838, boxers were allowed to **hit below the belt, head-butt, and bite without penalty**.

518 ➤ Sucker punches

Gambling scandals eroded the image of boxing in the 1930s, led by the shenanigans of Jim Norris. He was said to have "fixed" the Harry Thomas-Max Schmeling fight in 1937 and Jake Lamotta verses Billy Fox in 1946. Despite his fight fixing, **Norris went on to become president of the International Boxing Club** and to rule the televised boxing world in the 1950s.

519 ➤ Hope you're not in a hurry

An early version of baseball, called "rounders," was played without an umpire and with as many as fifteen men per side. Bases might be rocks or extra clothing, and the ball was typically an unraveled wool sock wound around a cork. **The winner was whichever team scored one hundred runs.**

520 ➤ Yer out! And unconscious!

Until the New York Knickerbockers began playing what we might recognize as baseball in 1845, **base runners had to be "plugged" or "plunked"—hit, often painfully, by a thrown ball—rather than simply tagged out.**

521 ➤ Steal a base? Why not steal the whole game?

Baseball, the new national pastime, was also a popular sport to bet on—inevitably leading to scandals and fixed games. In 1874, a sports magazine commented, "There is no sport now in vogue in which so much fraud prevails as in baseball. **Any professional baseball club will throw a game if there is money.** ... Horseracing is a pretty safe thing in comparison."

➤ Eight men out

Baseball's gambling problem hit bottom with the "Black Sox Scandal," in which eight players for the Chicago White Sox conspired with underworld figures to throw the 1919 World Series to the Cincinnati Reds. When the scandal was uncovered, **the players were banned for life.**

523 ➤ A new meaning to spitball

The 1910s in baseball were also notable as the "dead ball" era. The new ball was soft, cutting down on offensive pop, and discolored so it was harder to see as the pitcher released it. Hitters complained that **pitchers added to the ball's grimy look by dousing it with tobacco juice**.

524 ➤ Take me out to the ball game, if you can

The scarcity of goods essential to the war effort during World War II put a crimp in the nation's fun as well as its industry. Baseball suffered as balls low in rubber became dull and unresponsive, while **scant supplies of wood led to a shortage of bats**.

525 ➤ Who's on first?

The next shortage to hit America's pastime was of ballplayers themselves. By 1943, half the major leagues' ballplayers were in the military. Teams brought older players out of retirement, and **the St. Louis Browns even put a one-armed outfielder, Pete Gray, in the field**.

526 ➤ Game called for lack of ambulatory players

Early football games were infamous for their savage play and high injury rates. As many as **one-third of the players might be hurt in any given game**.

527 ➤ Taking a bullet for the team

Tossing around the football before the annual Thanksgiving feast sometimes meant taking your life in your hands—especially if you were a youngster whom police might view as a "juvenile delinquent." The social reformer Jacob Riis once wrote, "We have seen in New York **a boy shot down by a policeman for the heinous crime of playing football on the street** on Thanksgiving Day."

528 ➤ Sure, he can pass, but can he tackle?

Until the introduction of two-platoon football in 1941, **all eleven players had to play both offense and defense**—no substitutions allowed, except in case of injury.

529 ➤ Toot once for holding

The penalty flag wasn't introduced in football until 1941, and didn't become official until 1948. It was a brainstorm of Youngstown State coach Dwight Beede, who may have thought **a flag would be less raucous than the horns and whistles officials previously used to signal a penalty**.

530 ➤ Peachy keen idea, Coach!

Basketball, invented by James Naismith in 1891 to keep his gym class busy on a rainy day, originally used peach baskets instead of hoops and nets. Naismith didn't think to cut the bottom out of the basket, so **the ball had to be retrieved manually after each score**.

531 ➤ Is that a foul?

Basketball continued to use peach baskets—with the bottom knocked out—until 1906, when the metal hoop and backboard were introduced. The backboard proved necessary to **prevent fans behind the basket from reaching out and interfering with shots**.

532 ➤ Double, or maybe triple, dribbling

Dribbling wasn't initially part of basketball and, even when it was introduced, its utility was limited because the asymmetric balls—**the game originally used a ball similar to a football**—bounced unpredictably. Not until more uniform balls were manufactured in the 1950s did dribbling really catch on.

533 ➤ Whose side are you on?

The first form of hockey was field hockey. In the seventeenth and early eighteenth centuries field hockey was a chaotic and violent game played by competing villages with as many as one hundred players on a side. **The game might last for days, until so many players were injured that a halt was called**.

534 ➤ Peter Rabbit, meet Bobby Beaver

The first ice-hockey puck was supposedly **a piece of frozen beaver bladder.** Legend has it that a Canadian with the unlikely name of Pierre Lapin (Peter Rabbit) struck the bladder bit with a crooked stick he used to steady himself on the ice, and ice hockey was born.

535 ➤ Harder to say than it is to play

Major Walter Wingfield, who gave tennis its modern form, sought to patent the game in 1874 as **Sphairistike**, a Greek word meaning "ball game."

536 ➤ A hero to golf widows even today

King James II briefly banned the game of golf in 1457 **for reasons of national defense**: Golf, the king feared, was taking time away from practicing archery.

537 ➤ Titleist, it ain't

Affluent golfers in the seventeenth century upgraded from a simple wooden ball to a pricey leather alternative dubbed a "featherie" because it was stuffed with goose down or chicken feathers. Despite the price tag, featheries varied in size and weight and **might lose their feathers in the middle of a round.**

538 ➤ Does Tiger Woods know about this?

Never hook or slice again with the help of Hugh M. Rhind's golf-training device, patented in 1919. The device consisted of an **L-shaped pole that extended out over the golfer's head.** A second, smaller pole with an end like a shower head then dropped from the "L" to hold the golfer's head in place and keep him upright while swinging the club.

539 ➤ Let's see Michael Phelps handle that!

The revival of the Olympic Games in Athens in 1896 included the first Olympic swimming competition. But swimming pools were still a luxury, so the contest was held in the Bay of Zea on the Aegean Sea. Gold medalist Alfred Hoyos Guttman had to contend with **frigid water and waves up to twelve feet high.**

540 ➤ In a pinch, they could be used as anchors

Until about 1915, swimming wasn't viewed as a sport appropriate for women, and so their seaside recreation sometimes involved merely bobbing in the waves while holding a rope attached to a buoy. No actual swimming was possible, since **women's swimsuits might weigh more than twenty-two pounds**.

541 ➤ Me, Tarzan!

Men could actually go swimming in the ocean—as long as they kept their shirts on. The beaches of Atlantic City, New Jersey, for example, banned topless men until 1937 because the city didn't want "**gorillas on our beaches.**"

542 ➤ Keep off the grass

The first parks weren't built for people at all, but rather for **deer and other hunting prey**. In medieval times, the walls around the parks were designed to keep the critters inside and to keep out potential poachers, as well as others who might merely be out for a stroll.

543 ➤ Please don't sit on the headstones

Before urban parks became popular, **people who wanted to escape the crowded cities for a bit of green grass and fresh air went to cemeteries**. Going to the cemetery, even taking a picnic, became a popular pastime.

544 ➤ Making themselves at home

New York City's Central Park, designed in 1857 and largely completed by 1873, was one of the nation's first large city parks. But even this showplace quickly fell into disrepair, as **squatters moved in and started using Central Park's lakes as a giant toilet and trash can**. By 1875, fear of malarial fever led many to avoid the park.

545 ➤ If you want to see one, get a nickel!

Hunting, not only for sport but for food, was integral to life in the United States from the earliest colonial days. Sometimes, though, it got a little out of hand: Between 1870 and 1890, **some fifteen million buffalo roaming the Great Plains were hunted and killed, almost leading to the buffalo's extinction**—only a few hundred remained. Most were hunted only for their skins, with the rest of the animals' carcasses left to rot. The U.S. Army, as well as the railroads, actively encouraged the sporting slaughter, to deprive indigenous tribes of food and to remove the huge animals as a threat to trains.

546 ➤ Itching for stardom

Yes, there really were flea circuses—with real fleas. These attractions were first promoted as early as 1833 and were a popular carnival show through the 1920s. In some small U.S. towns, flea circuses continued to perform into the 1960s. As **improved sanitation made it increasingly hard to find enough fleas,** the attractions began to fade away.

547 ➤ You have to keep the talent happy
The demise of flea circuses may have been a relief to their human ringmasters, who had to **feed the tiny performers with their own blood**—typically, twice a day, for fifteen to thirty minutes per feeding.

548 ➤ Ready for their close-up
The "performers" in flea circuses weren't actually trained, but were simply sorted into fleas that jumped and those that preferred to run. **Tiny harnesses of thin gold wire were then fitted about the insects and attached to the various "circus" props** that the fleas—strong for their size—would manipulate. Jumping fleas would appear to kick a small ball; actually, they would be trying to escape from the ball, but the harness caused them to push the ball instead. Running fleas could be made to pull small carts or rotate wheels. Female fleas were said to be better performers than the males.

549 ➤ Music to the ears of a flea-bitten dog
There were also flea "orchestras," of a sort. **Fleas would be glued to the base of the performance area and tiny musical instruments would in turn be glued to the fleas.** When the base was heated, the frantic fleas—trying to escape—would appear to be playing the instruments.

550 ➤ Of course, this was before they had WWE
A popular sport into the early twentieth century was "rat-baiting." Similar to cock-fighting or dogfighting, rat-baiting involved a less even contest: Rats were placed in a pit and then **spectators would wager on how long it would take a terrier to kill all the rats.**

551 ➤ Taking your chances

Gambling was illegal in most parts of the United States until legalized by Nevada in 1931, but that didn't mean it wasn't popular. In New York City alone in 1870, it's estimated gamblers could take their pick of **2,500 illegal gambling joints**.

552 ➤ What's French for "look out!"?

The first roller rink was opened in France by Jean Garcin. An enthusiastic proponent of the new sport, Garcin patented a skate design in 1828, gave lessons and wrote a book, *Le Vrai Patineur* (The True Skater). He perhaps should have given more lessons, however, as **his rink soon shut down after an epidemic of injuries**.

553 ➤ Nothing to do but stare at the wall

Fun in rural areas was hard to find back when. Growing up in a cabin in Ohio around 1850, William Dean Howells—later a renowned author, editor, and critic—entertained himself by **reading, over and over, an old copy of a New York newspaper his father had used as wallpaper**.

554 ➤ Getting airtime before radio

You think you have a tough job: The popularity of sing-along sheet music, which saw popular songs selling over a million copies in the early 1900s, led to "song pluggers." These **traveling musicians carried their pianos with them on horse-drawn carts**, performing popular songs in hopes that listeners would purchase the sheet music.

555

➤ Never say never

Much as the *Titanic* was promoted as unsinkable, Chicago's 1,602-seat Iroquois Theater was touted as "absolutely fireproof." So imagine the surprise of the more than two thousand patrons who overfilled the theater on December 28, 1903, for the matinee of *Mr. Bluebeard*: Sparks from an electric arc lamp ignited a backstage fire, which the new theater's still-unfinished sprinkler system could not extinguish. When Eddie Foy Sr., the star of the play, called from on stage for the asbestos curtain to be dropped, nothing happened—the promised fireproof curtain did not exist. As the scenery burst into blames, the audience broke into "a mad, animal-like stampede." **Bodies piled up six feet high at the exits**, while the theater's grand marble staircase filled twenty bodies deep with suffocating patrons. The final body count was 602, mostly women and children.

556 ➤ Great show, if you survive it

Going up in flames was actually a common hazard of attending the theater. Part of the problem was the proliferation of limelights (as in the phrase "in the limelight"), in which a small amount of quicklime (calcium oxide) was exposed to an intense flame. The resulting bright, white light was perfect for illuminating a stage—as well as for setting the whole place on fire, because of the heat that was also generated. **During one decade alone, more than four hundred U.S. theaters were destroyed by fire.**

557 ➤ A movie seems like a safe bet on a snowy day

But it wasn't just fire that folks in search of entertainment had to fear. A blizzard that blanketed the eastern United States in January 1922 delivered such heavy snow that the Knickerbocker Theater in New York City collapsed under the wintry weight, **killing 120 moviegoers.**

558 ➤ Where dreams go up in smoke

The Dreamland Park at Coney Island was among the first amusement parks to be wired for electricity and illuminated by electric lights. But in 1911, when bursting light bulbs and a spilled bucket of hot pitch being used for repairs set the "Hell Gate" ride on fire, **the blaze swiftly spread through the grounds.** Most of the buildings were made of thin lath frames covered with a moldable mixture of plaster of paris and hemp fiber—all highly flammable. Chaos ensued as panicked crowds fled and some of the sideshow lions and tigers escaped. By the time the fire from the ironically named "Hell Gate" was extinguished, Dreamland Park was destroyed.

559 ➤ Beat out the flames with a tiny drink umbrella!

Then there were nightclubs, like Boston's Cocoanut Grove, which was packed to twice its capacity on November 28, 1942, when a busboy's dropped match ignited an artificial palm tree. The club's tropical décor was as flammable as it was faux. **Panicked crowds crushed one hundred patrons to death in the doorway,** and 491 people in all died.

560 ➤ The greatest blaze on earth

Canvas circus tents were often treated with paraffin and gasoline, making "The Greatest Show on Earth" an inferno waiting to happen. A 1944 blaze in Hartford, Connecticut, **claimed 168 lives and burned or injured another 174 attendees** at the Ringling Brothers circus. Many lives were saved, however, by the quick thinking of the circus' bandleader who, seeing flames, struck up "The Stars and Stripes Forever"—a circus signal for an emergency.

561 ➤ Her ankle really stole the scene

The 1903 silent movie *The Gay Shoe Clerk* wasn't scandalous for the reason you think: While showing a "fresh young shoe clerk" trying a pair of high-heeled slippers on a young lady, the movie zoomed in on the attractive patron's leg. According to promotional materials, "Her dress is slightly raised, showing a shapely ankle, and the clerk's hands begin to tremble, making it difficult for him to tie the slipper." The clerk nonetheless "makes rapid progress" and is soon shown kissing the patron. But it wasn't the kiss that scandalized movie audiences so much as **the first on-screen depiction of a woman's bare ankle**.

562 ➤ He really blew that line

Perhaps inspired by word balloons in the early comic strips, C.F. Pidgin's 1917 patented invention used an **inflatable tube coming out of a movie actor's mouth with his or her lines written on it**. Fortunately for actors' dignity, talkies came along in the 1920s.

563 ➤ The ultimate diet pill

In the 1930s, jockeys desperate to lose weight for horse racing would **swallow a capsule containing a tapeworm egg**. When the egg hatched, the tapeworm would consume the contents of the jockey's stomach.

564 ➤ Maybe the tow trucks should have raced

The wartime closure of the Indianapolis 500 speedway proved tough on the track, which deteriorated from disuse and lack of maintenance. When racing resumed at last in 1946, **twenty-four cars failed to finish**.

565 ➤ White lightning

NASCAR was born from races between the souped-up cars used by moonshiners to outrun "revenooers" during Prohibition. When not staying ahead of the law (literally), **"runners" of bootleg liquor held informal races for bragging rights**.

566 ➤ They're still reviewing the results

The inaugural Daytona 500 in 1959 **took sixty-one hours after the race was over to declare a winner**. "Big Bill France" spent that time scrutinizing news footage of the race before declaring Lee Petty the victor.

567 ➤ Was he catching a wave to a dinner party?

Why waste time paddling out to "hang 10"? In 1948, Hollywood inventor Joe Gilpin showed off his **motorized surfboard**, which he demonstrated while wearing a formal suit, tie, dress shoes, and hat, and smoking a cigarette. There may have been some aspects of surfing that Gilpin didn't quite grasp.

568 ➤ The smell of money going down the drain

It sounds like a joke, but there really was such a thing as Smell-o-Vision. Mike Todd Jr., son of the movie mogul, funded an elaborate system in which **the film reel triggered the release of bottled scents, synchronized with the action onscreen**. *Scent of Mystery*, released in 1960, was the only movie to utilize Smell-o-Vision. Audiences thought it, well, stunk.

12 NO-GO

← Transportation flops and detours →

569 ➤ Where are the brakes on this thing?

Steamboats were the first great leap forward in mechanized transportation. But the new era of steamboat travel had barely begun before its first great collision in 1837, when the *Monmouth* ran into the *Tremont* near Profit Island on the Mississippi River. **The steamboat crash killed some three hundred passengers and crew.**

570 ➤ Caution, wet paint

Not even giving a steamboat a fresh coat of paint and varnish was entirely safe—not if the painters left turpentine too close to the boiler. Not long after the spiffed-up steamer *Erie* left Buffalo for Chicago in 1841, the turpentine exploded. **The fresh paint and varnish spread the flames like napalm, killing 242 people.** Many were burned alive, while others drowned when overloaded lifeboats capsized or they were crushed in the paddle wheels.

571 ➤ Some corners shouldn't be cut

The potential dangers of shipboard paint failed to sink in, apparently, as in 1904 combustible materials in a paint locker combined with a freshly painted exterior to cause one of the most strange and horrendous steamboat fires ever—the tragedy of the *General Slocum*, for which its captain went to Sing Sing prison. Most of the paddle wheel steamer's 1,500 passengers for the day-long excursion around New York City were members of a German-immigrant church. Few spoke English, so their warnings about a fire and cries for help went unheeded. Not that it would have mattered: The *General Slocum's* **life preservers had been stuffed with sawdust and metal rods so they'd pass a weight test, and its lifeboats were wired immovably in place.** Compounding the disaster, Captain William Van Schaick ran the ship aground with its stern in thirty feet of water—upriver from the harbor, instead of returning to port. Then he and most of the crew fled, as 1,021 passengers perished.

572 ➤ Anybody got a protractor?

The Erie Canal, called "Clinton's Folly" by skeptics after New York Governor DeWitt Clinton, was the young nation's most ambitious engineering project. Yet the United States at the time had **not a single native-born engineer who had ever worked on a canal.**

573 ➤ Third time's not the charm

Horace Lawson Hunley, the inventor of the first combat submarine, can't be faulted for having too little faith in his invention. The eponymous *CSS Hunley* had already sunk twice during routine exercises in 1863 when the Confederate inventor took command. **The submarine sank a third time**, drowning Hunley and seven crew members.

574 ➤ Short-lived freedom

"The most staggering and appalling marine disaster in history," according to the *Washington Times,* was the 1865 explosion of the packet steamer *Sultana.* Packed with former Union prisoners of war freed from Confederate camps, the steamer suddenly exploded and sank. Estimates of the **death toll range from 1,450 to 2,200.**

575 ➤ A whale of a tale

Did anyone ever actually **fall off a ship, get swallowed by a whale, and live to tell about it?** One real-life Jonah, according to some accounts, was a seaman aboard *The Star of the East* named James Bartley, whose whaling boat capsized while hunting off the Falkland Islands in 1891. A fellow crewman drowned, but Bartley's body wasn't found—until the sperm whale was killed and butchered, revealing the missing seaman, unconscious, inside. Bartley enjoyed a full recovery from his ordeal, except that his exposed skin was bleached "the color of parchment" by the whale's gastric juices.

576

➤ He should have kept the movie rights

We can't forget the *Titanic*. You know the story of the iceberg rendezvous that sank the "unsinkable" White Star Line luxury liner, claiming 1,517 lives. But did you know that **the April 1912 disaster was eerily presaged in a book by Morgan Robertson published in 1898**? In Robertson's novel, titled *Futility*, an ocean liner named *Titan* sinks on its maiden voyage—in April— after striking an iceberg.

577 ➤ Something doesn't add up here

The *Titanic* had 2,207 passengers and crew onboard its doomed maiden voyage, but **only enough lifeboats for 1,178**. Some desperate men disguised themselves as women to get a space in the "women and children first" lifeboats. A director of the White Star Line that owned the ship leaped over the rail into the last lifeboat as it was being launched, to save himself, as his customers were left to die.

578 ➤ Who would call at this hour?

Among the ships that might have helped rescue passengers and crew from the *Titanic* was the *Californian*, which was only five minutes from the sinking vessel. **But the *Californian* had turned its radio off for the night.** When the captain saw signal rockets shot off by the *Titanic* as distress signals, he assumed they were fireworks from a party aboard the luxury liner and went to bed.

579 ✈ They never knew what hit them

Compared to the terrifying ordeal of those aboard the *Titanic*, the 1,042 passengers and crew who perished when the *Empress of Ireland* went down in 1914 might count themselves lucky: **Most drowned in their sleep.** A coal-carrying boat emerged from a fog bank and plowed into the passenger liner, ripping a hole half the length of the *Empress* and sending it to the bottom in just fifteen minutes.

580 ✈ For the yachtsman who has everything

Even after steam replaced wind as the power for most vessels, some inventors didn't stop trying to improve the sailing experience. In 1916, Edward Niklaus Breitung patented a **windmill attachment for ships**, designed to act as an additional sail as well as to generate electricity on board.

581 ✈ Inventing the train wreck

The United States had less than one hundred miles of railroad tracks in 1830, but it wasn't long before people started dying on them. The earliest recorded train wreck deaths occurred in 1833, when a Camden & Amboy **train derailed at twenty miles an hour** near Hightstown, New Jersey, killing two passengers. Among the twenty-four others injured was Cornelius Vanderbilt, whose broken leg led him to swear off trains for the next thirty years. (He would, however, later buy up several railroad companies and consolidate them into the New York Central & Hudson River Railroad Company, one of America's first giant corporations.)

582 ➤ A game of chicken?

Other notorious train wrecks occurred when **two onrushing trains simply collided head-on.** In the Great Train Wreck of 1856, the deadliest railroad disaster in the world up to that time, the Shakamaxon and Aramingo locomotives ran right into each other near Fort Washington, Pennsylvania, killing about sixty people and injuring another one hundred.

583 ➤ We hope he was thankful to catch the next train

In 1867, another famous multimillionaire, John D. Rockefeller, narrowly escaped death in the "Angola Horror" train wreck in Angola, New York: His bags arrived at the station in time to catch the doomed New York Express for Buffalo, but Rockefeller was too late. Lucky for him, as the Lake Shore Railway train derailed crossing the Big Sister Creek gorge. Most of the approximate fifty dead were passengers in the last car, which plunged forty feet down an ice-covered slope, pinning the occupants between two stoves that kept the car warm. When kerosene from lamps hit the hot coals from the stoves, **the hapless riders trapped inside were burned alive.**

584 ➤ Bridge to nowhere

Bridge failure was to blame for the Ashtabula River train wreck of 1876, which would, for a time, be the worst such crash in American history. As the Lake Shore and Michigan Southern Railway train plowed through an Ohio snowstorm, **the bridge over the Ashtabula River broke beneath it, toppling eleven railcars some seventy feet into the ravine.** Of 159 passengers and crew on board, sixty-four were injured and ninety-two killed by the crash or subsequent fires. At least one of the men who'd designed the flawed bridge later committed suicide.

585 ➤ If Train No. 4 leaves at 7 A.M....

It proved tough to keep that "Great Train Wreck" title, however, as the Great Train Wreck of 1918 in Nashville would become the deadliest railroad accident in American history. The No. 4 passenger train of the Nashville, Chattanooga and St. Louis Railway left Nashville at 7 A.M. on July 9. The No. 1 from Memphis to Nashville, however, was running about a half hour late. At 7:20 A.M., the two **collided head-on at speeds of fifty to sixty miles an hour** along the "Dutchman's Curve," killing 101 people and injuring 171 others.

586 ➤ Death by iron horse

You were safer in a war zone than having anything to do with America's railroads, according to a calculation by the *New York Post*. Trains caused about as many deaths between June 1898 and 1900, the newspaper concluded, as the **British Army suffered in three years of fighting in the Boer War.**

587 ➤ I hear a train a-comin'

Railroads killed plenty of people who weren't even riding on the trains. Railroad grade crossings were marked only by an *X*—not the flashing lights and crossing buck of today. **In one year alone, Chicago recorded 330 railroad-crossing fatalities**, and once totaled sixteen deaths in a single accident, for which no one was ever held accountable.

588 ➤ Boiled beef, anyone?

Then there was the problem of stray animals on the railroad tracks. Going the "cow catcher" one better was Lafayette Willson Page's 1884 invention of a water gun mounted on the front of the locomotive. The device would channel **hot water from the engine's boiler into a stream shot at critters on the tracks**, encouraging them to vamoose.

589 ➤ Put out an APB on Snidely Whiplash!

The melodrama notion of **tying a hapless victim to a railroad track** may have originated in fiction (where it was popularized in an 1867 play by Augustin Daly, *Under the Gaslight*), but copycats soon tried it for real. In 1874, *The New York Times* reported that a Frenchman named Gardner was robbed and then roped to railroad tracks. He had mostly wriggled free when a train roared past and severed his still-tethered left leg below the knee. Monsieur Gardner lived long enough to describe his ordeal before dying of his injuries.

590 ➤ The fast and the furious, eighteenth-century style

Before the motorcar—with its own panoply of hazards—horse-drawn vehicles brought constant carnage to streets and roadways. In 1720, **"furiously driven carts and coaches" were cited as the leading cause of death in London.**

591 ➤ A fact not to trample on

As late as 1867 in New York City, horses were the cause of an average **four pedestrian deaths a week**.

592 ➤ Does this mare come with air bags?

In the nineteenth-century heyday of horse-powered transportation, according to the National Safety Council, the rate of **transportation-related fatalities was ten times the rate of today's car traffic deaths**.

593 ➤ Made for midnight rides

When horses were the main mode of transportation, it was cumbersome to carry a lantern to light your (and the horse's) way. So why didn't anybody think of the **Horse Head Lamp** sooner? The invention patented in 1879 by L.G. Macauley enabled a road lantern to be affixed to the top of a horse's head.

594 ➤ Going nowhere fast

Traffic through already-crowded New York City in the 1890s was further impeded by streets narrowed by parked wagons, unharnessed from their horses—beneath which littering residents tossed their trash. When an 1895 ordinance called for abandoned wagons to be towed, **teamsters frustrated enforcement by removing one or more wheels from their parked wagons**.

595 ➤ Life in the fast lane?

Electric trolleys were supposed to go far faster than their horse-drawn predecessors, with a top speed of over twenty miles an hour. But since there was no way to get other horse traffic out of the path of the trolleys, the **electric streetcars crawled along at a horse's clip-clop pace and seldom approached their rated speed**.

596 ➤ Not exactly Henry Ford

Most experts agree that the first road vehicle to move under its own power was invented by a French artillery captain, Nicholas-Joseph Cugnot, in 1769. Dubbed the *fardier*, Cugnot's creation used the newfangled pressurized steam engine—developed by James Watt that very year—to propel a cart. On its first excursion, however, the fardier struck and knocked down a wall; designed to ferry cannons, the vehicle also tended to tip over forward unless counterbalanced with a cannon in the rear. The second and final fardier, in 1770, **weighed four tons and reached two miles an hour.**

597 ➤ The hat is what put it over the top

Inventors Zadoc Dederick and Isaac Grass somehow managed to get a patent in 1868 for their design of **a steam carriage in the shape of a top-hatted man smoking a pipe and pulling a cart**. Stylish, certainly, but it inexplicably failed to catch on.

598 ➤ The human hamster

As bicycles grew in popularity, inventors tried putting their own, er, spin on human-powered transportation. In 1885, John O. Lose patented **an inside-out unicycle** in which the cyclist sits inside a giant wheel, not unlike a hamster. The cyclist (protected from the elements by an umbrella inside the wheel) pedals a small interior wheel that in turn drives the large one.

599 ➤ From passenger to pedestrian to corpse
The first person to be run over and killed by an automobile had, until an instant before, been riding in the car. In 1869, Mary Ward, an Irish naturalist and illustrator, was tooling about with her husband in an experimental steam-powered vehicle built by her cousins. The 1865 Red Flag Act had imposed a **speed limit of two miles an hour in town and four miles an hour in the country**, effectively killing the UK's fledgling motorcar industry. But some amateurs, like Ward's cousins, built their own—which was evidently fast enough to throw her out of the vehicle on a sharp turn. She was crushed under the iron wheels, which broke her neck, and died almost instantly.

600 ➤ The same thing happened to a tortoise & a hare
In 1871, J.W. Carhart, a Wisconsin physics professor, built a working steam car that inspired the state to sponsor a two-hundred-mile race in 1878 with a ten-thousand-dollar prize. **Only two of seven entries made it to the starting line**, and the faster of those broke down before the finish, leaving the prize to an Oshkosh model that averaged six miles an hour.

601 ➤ Moving at the speed of a stiff breeze
When automobiles first hit the highways, **there were no speed limits**, but cars couldn't go very fast anyway. By 1906, fifteen states had adopted speed limits—of twenty miles per hour.

602 ⤙ Hanging speeders out to dry

As automobiles became faster and more popular, police invented the speed trap. The first were quite literally traps: **Police strung ropes across the road to catch speeders**, who responded by fitting the front of their cars with blades to slice right through.

603 ⤙ The first speed bumps

As speeders frustrated police efforts at early speed traps, authorities countered by stretching wire cables across the road, or simply **placing logs in the middle of the highway**.

604 ⤙ The old nag's still good for something

One deterrent to speeding was the awful nature of roads, which spurred thousands of public meetings between 1890 and 1916. The holler of "Get a horse!" was no joke, as **a horse was often the only way to haul a stranded automobile out of ruts, mud, and ditches**.

605 ⤙ I call shotgun

"Rumble seats," popular in automobiles of the late 1920s and the 1930s, added both passenger seating and wind-in-your-hair fun to roadsters. The seats folded out from the rear end of a car and were **like riding in a shallow, open trunk**— and just as dangerous. Passengers in a rumble seat had no protection from the elements, much less seat belts.

606 ⤙ Buckle up for brain trauma

Although the seat belt was patented by George Cayley in 1885, it was slow to win acceptance in automobiles—and early seat belts probably did more harm than good. The idea for modern retractable seat belts came from a neurologist, Dr. C. Hunter Shelden, who was appalled at the head injuries he saw come in through emergency rooms. Shelden found that **primitive seat belts were actually contributors to the brain injuries**.

607 ➤ Tire sales would have been cut in half!

If bicycles and motorcycles can ride on only two wheels, why not automobiles? Ford gave it a try in 1961 with the Gyron, **a two-wheeled "gyrocar" stabilized by gyroscopes**. The Gyron could hold a passenger as well as the driver, seated side by side rather than in-line as on a motorcycle. When parked, two small legs popped out to keep the Gyron from tipping over. Alas, the Gyron never went into production.

608 ➤ Your tire's burnt out again

Another 1961 innovation in the automotive industry that inexplicably failed to catch on was Goodyear's **illuminated tires**. Made from a single piece of synthetic rubber, the tires were brightly lit by bulbs mounted inside the wheel rim, which made the whole tire glow. A promotional photo suggested one handy use, showing a woman adjusting her stockings by the glow of a tire.

609 ➤ Chain reaction

As automobile traffic grew, so did smog—and inevitably the two combined in the 1973 New Jersey Turnpike smog accident. Actually, "accidents" would be more accurate, as **the pileups that killed nine people, injured thirty-nine and involved sixty-six vehicles began at 11:20 P.M. and continued until 2:45 the next morning.** One car after another would crash into the smog-shrouded accident scene, adding to the wreckage.

610 ➤ What goes up...

The dubious distinction of being the first person killed in an air crash belongs to Jean-François Pilâtre de Rozier, **way back in 1785**. His balloon crashed when he and a partner were attempting to cross the English Channel.

611 ➤ Wilbur, we have a problem

Famed airplane co-inventor Orville Wright nearly experienced the downside of the Wright Brothers' creation fatally and firsthand in 1908 when a plane he was piloting developed mechanical problems and crashed in Maryland. **Wright survived but his passenger, Lieutenant T.E. Selfridge, was killed** in one of the first fatal airplane crashes.

612 ➤ It doesn't take a rocket scientist

Another aviation pioneer who wound up a victim of his own invention was rocket scientist Max Valier. After helping invent liquid-fueled rocket engines in the 1920s, in 1930 Valier was working on an **alcohol-fueled rocket that exploded** on his test bench, killing him instantly.

613 ➤ Up in flames

Dirigible enthusiasts might have seen the fiery writing on the wall when a hydrogen-filled airship, the R101, was destroyed in a flaming crash during a storm in France in 1930, **killing forty-eight passengers and crew**. But dirigible designers failed to fully appreciate the dangers of filling a giant balloon with highly flammable hydrogen until greater tragedies unfolded.

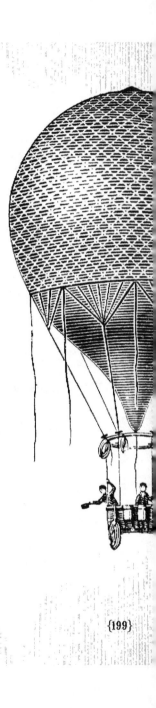

614 ➤ Maybe man was not meant to float

Three years later, another airship, the 758-foot USS *Akron*, was struck by lightning after lifting off from Lakehurst, New Jersey, for a routine flight. Although the dirigible did not immediately catch fire, it did **crash into the ocean some twenty miles off the coast.** Only four of the seventy-seven crew members survived, rescued after a passing tanker spotted the eerie glow of flames from the airship's wreckage.

615 ➤ Oh, the humanity!

The risks of flying hydrogen-filled dirigibles didn't truly hit home, however, until the 804-foot *Hindenburg* crashed in a ball of fire, again at Lakehurst, New Jersey, in 1937. **The destruction of the world's largest dirigible killed thirty-five of the ninety-seven people on board**—luckily, well below the airship's maximum capacity of 158 passengers and crew.

616 ➤ Well, they both start with H...

Ironically, although the *Hindenburg* had been built by Nazi Germany as a demonstration of its technological prowess, **prewar tensions had cut off supplies of strategically important, nonflammable helium to keep the airship aloft.** Instead, the *Hindenburg* was filled with seven million cubic feet of hydrogen. It took just thirty-two seconds to burn after a small flame shot out of the tail fin during a routine mooring. The exact cause of the blaze has never been determined.

617

➤ It's a train! It's a plane!

The Aerowagon, invented by Valerian Abakovsky, was supposed to **combine a train with the power and propeller action of an aircraft.** Abakovsky and a bevy of government officials took it for a test run in 1921. On the routine trip, the Aerowagon derailed at high speed, killing its twenty-five-year-old inventor and everyone else on board.

618 ➤ By land and air

Another ill-fated transportation pioneer was Henry Smolinski, who tried to **build a flying car by strapping the wings and tail from a Cessna airplane onto an automobile.** During a 1973 test flight in California, the car separated from the airplane assemblage and plummeted earthward, killing Smolinski and a passenger. Perhaps he shouldn't have used a Ford Pinto.

619 ➤ If it walks like a duck...

Take a pair of giant foam "shoes," add two poles with ends like duck feet for propulsion, and you have inventor M.W. Hulton's 1962 **Sea-Shoes.** Like snow skis, except floating on the water, the invention let wearers waddle along without getting (very) wet.

620 ➤ A real spring in your step

On dry land, you could simply bounce along on **Spring Shoes**, patented by Harry Brant and Henry Turner in 1920. A large spring attached to the bottom of each shoe propelled the wearer with every step.

13 LIFE IN A STATE OF NATURE

← Wild things and natural (and unnatural) disasters ⇢

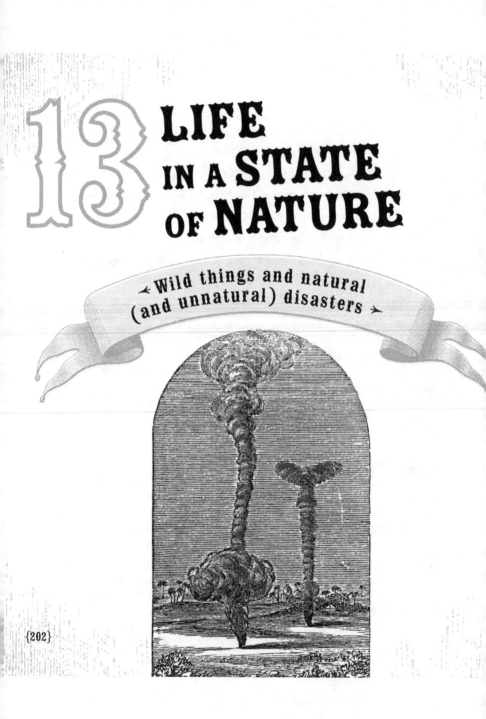

621 ➤ Whole lotta shakin' goin' on

Though Americans associate earthquakes with California, the country's first great quakes took place in Missouri. From December 16, 1811, to February 7, 1812, the town of New Madrid recorded 1,874 quakes and aftershocks. The **Mississippi River flowed backward for hundreds of miles** and two new waterfalls were formed.

622 ➤ Did the earth move for you, too?

The Missouri quakes of 1811–12 were felt far beyond the epicenter, shaking 1.5 million square miles. The movement of the **earth caused church bells to ring as far away as Charleston, South Carolina**, and rattled chandeliers in Washington, D.C.

623 ➤ Talk about a "groundswell!"

For sheer destruction per minute, it's hard to top the San Francisco earthquake of 1906. The quake, measuring 8.5 on the Richter Scale, took just two minutes to ravage the Bay Area with "earth waves" up to three feet high that turned boulders into projectiles and toppled redwoods. **Cracks opened in the earth, swallowed livestock whole, then closed up again**, sometimes leaving nothing above ground but the tail of a cow.

624 ➤ A bad day for insurance companies, too

Fires followed the San Francisco quake, **consuming property at a rate of one million dollars every ten minutes**. Between the quake and fire, three out of five homes were seriously damaged and 490 city blocks were wiped out. The final toll was some seven hundred deaths, more than a quarter million left homeless, and 28,000 buildings destroyed.

625 ➤ Say aloha to this!

In 1946, an undersea quake in the Aleutian Islands launched a **one-hundred-foot-high seismic wave that headed for Hawaii at five hundred miles an hour**. When it reached the islands—without warning—the waves were still fifty feet high, destroying one thousand structures and killing 179 people.

626 ➤ Extinct? I'll show you extinct!

History is full of erupting volcanoes, but few can match the human carnage of Vesuvius' 79 A.D. destruction of Pompeii and Herculaneum. Residents thought the volcano, which had been quiet for thousands of years, was extinct. So imagine their surprise when "a cloud of unusual size and appearance" materialized above Vesuvius, and it began to rain hot ash at a rate of six inches an hour. Many fled, but sixteen thousand were trapped by the "fearful black cloud rent by forked and quivering bursts of flame." Both towns were **buried beneath fifteen to twenty feet of ash**, where they remained until excavations began in 1748.

627 ➤ Forecast: Blizzards, famine, and riots

Fine dust thrown into the atmosphere by the eruption of Mount Tambora in Java, half a world away, turned 1816 into "the year without a summer" in America and Europe. (That explanation would not be puzzled out, however, until 1920.) A blizzard dumped twenty inches of snow on parts of the northeastern United States in June, and killing frosts left fields barren of crops. In the resulting famine, **people resorted to eating pigeons, groundhogs, and stray cats**, while English mobs armed with iron spikes and "Bread or Blood" signs looted towns in search of even a crust to eat.

628 ➤ Not exactly a Caribbean vacation

In modern times, the worst volcanic disaster of the twentieth century was the 1902 eruption of Mount Pelée in Martinique. Lava burst out of the volcano and reached the city of St. Pierre, already clogged with refugees from the volcanic threat, in less than a minute. In all, **more than thirty thousand people are thought to have died from Mount Pelée's wrath**.

629 ➤ The best of all possible worlds—really?

The earthquake that struck Lisbon on All Saint's Day in 1755 not only claimed nearly fifty thousand lives but shook the faith of Europe. Voltaire fictionalized the quake in his satire *Candide* as a mockery of the naïve belief we live in "the best of all possible worlds." The nonfictional **earthquake opened a fifteen-foot fissure in the center of Lisbon**, toppled cathedrals onto worshippers, and caused a fifty-foot-high tsunami that killed ten thousand people across the sea in Morocco. Subsequent fires consumed two hundred artistic masterpieces and eighteen thousand rare books and maps used by Portuguese explorers, and finished the work of destroying all but three thousand of the city's twenty thousand buildings. Convinced that the disaster was a punishment from God, priests combed the ruins for heretics to burn.

630 ➤ Don't order the rye bread, tovarisch

A deadly fungus that infected rye bread killed twenty thousand Russians in a 1720 outbreak of ergotism. Also called "St. Anthony's fire," **the fungus causes convulsions, seizures, diarrhea, itching, headaches, hallucinations similar to those induced by LSD, nausea, and vomiting**. Those convulsive symptoms are followed by a dry gangrene, the loss of affected tissues and, if untreated by vasodilators unknown to the eighteenth century, death. Some have blamed the delusions that led to the Salem witchcraft trials on an earlier outbreak of ergotism.

631

➤ Look out below!

The first recorded deaths by hailstone in the United States occurred in 1784 when a thunderstorm hit Winnsboro, South Carolina. Hailstones as big as **nine inches around killed several slaves** caught out in the storm.

632 ➤ Something's eating at me

Winter's early arrival spelled disaster for many seeking their fortune in California's Gold Rush, most famously the ill-fated Donner Party. Heavy snow in late October 1846 trapped the ninety pioneers as they attempted to cross the Sierra Nevadas. **Only forty-eight would reach Sutter's Fort**, with some of those who perished becoming victims of cannibalism.

633 ➤ Snowy seas

In the Northeastern United States, they still talk about the "Great White Hurricane" of March 1888, whose **fifteen- to twenty-foot-high snow drifts shut down traffic**. At least four hundred people were killed, including one hundred or more seamen stranded on two hundred ships when the blizzard reached the ocean.

634 ➤ What would Pharaoh do?

In a plague of biblical proportions, an invading army of Rocky Mountain **locusts gobbled up the entire harvest of the Dakota Territory** in 1867. Clouds of locusts more than one hundred miles across blackened the sky, and most of the damage was done in a single day.

635 ➤ And this was before they had Raid

1875 was the true "year of the locust" across the central United States, when an un-precedented hatch estimated in the trillions began a hungry march from Colorado, Wyoming, and Montana eastward into farm country. One observer calculated **a swarm of locusts that took five days to pass** over Plattsmouth, Nebraska, was 1,800 miles long, and 110 miles wide. Another observer likened their flight to "an immense snowstorm, extending from the ground to a height at which our visual organs perceive them only as minute, darting scintillations."

636 ➤ Stop bugging me!

When the 1875 hordes of locusts landed and tried to take flight again, their num-bers were so thick that the locusts' wings got entangled with each other "and **they would drop to the ground again in a matted mass.**"

637 ➤ A clean sweep

In areas that got "grasshoppered" that spring and early summer of 1875, the locusts left behind land "as bare of vegetation as in midwinter" or looking as if the fields had been scorched by fire. One Missouri farmer watched **fifteen acres of corn get consumed in just three hours**: "They mowed it down close to the ground just as if a mowing machine had cut it." Except for a few jagged pieces of milkweed, "one might travel for days by buggy and find everything eaten off, even to underbrush in the woods."

638 ➤ Don't stand in one place too long

When the crops were all eaten, the 1875 horde of locusts started chomping on fence posts, ax handles, cloth, leather stirrups, bridles, gloves, paper, tree bark, even the clothing on people's backs. The hungry bugs would **eat the wool right off live sheep.**

639 ➤ Slip-sliding away

The locusts of 1875 continued to cause trouble even after they finally died. The **oil from crushed insects on railroad tracks could stop a train**, especially on an upward grade.

640 ➤ Hope you like your steak well-done

The 1871 Great Chicago Fire, the most destructive in U.S. history, consumed three and a third square miles, killed more than 250 people and left ninety thousand homeless. The blaze really did begin at a barn belonging to the O'Leary family, though the legend that a cow kicked over a lantern is probably apocryphal. Ironically, **the O'Leary house beside the barn was not among the 17,500 buildings burned.**

641 ➤ Where are those 10,000 lakes when you need them?

Whipped by winds, a 1918 wildfire in northern Minnesota and Wisconsin burned ten thousand square miles of forest and wiped out twenty-one towns, killing eight hundred people. A train packed with people fleeing the fire pulled out of Cloquet, Minnesota, in such a close call that **flames lapped at the cars and the heat blew out the windows**.

642 ➤ Dam it all!

The phrase "when the dam breaks" is not just metaphorical. The famous Johnstown Flood in 1889 was caused when a dam on the Conemaugh River, fourteen miles up in the Allegheny Mountains, gave way. A **wall of water hit the Pennsylvania town at fifty miles an hour**, killing more than two thousand people.

643 ➤ Watery wake-up call

In 1928, the 185-foot-high Saint Francis Dam holding back billions of gallons in a five-mile reservoir in San Francisquito Canyon, north of Los Angeles, became weakened by heavy rains and gave way on two sides early one morning. The seventy-foot-high wall of water roared through the Santa Clara River Valley at a rate of 500,000 cubic feet per second. The 350 people killed by the flood—**most of them crushed by boulders and debris**—had no warning as the waters took them in their beds.

644

➤ Auntie Em, Auntie Em!

In March 1925, the deadliest tornado to date in the United States left a three-hundred-mile trail of destruction through Missouri, Illinois, and Indiana, killing nearly seven hundred people in a span of about five hours. In DeSoto, Illinois, the **rapid change in air pressure as the tornado struck caused a schoolhouse to simply explode**. Among the five hundred residents of Parrish, Illinois, only three escaped injury or death. One victim in Princeton, Indiana, was found sucked halfway up the chimney of her house.

645 ➤ Five minutes of fury

Another tornado, in September 1927, took just **five minutes to kill eighty-five people, injure some 1,300 more, and destroy 1,800 homes** in St. Louis. Compounding the terror, witnesses reported seeing "sheets of fire" from the accompanying violent electrical storm.

646 ➤ No place is safe!

New England doesn't expect tornadoes, so the twister that killed ninety people in Worcester, Massachusetts, in 1953 was as shocking as it was lethal. About **four thousand buildings were destroyed in a matter of minutes**.

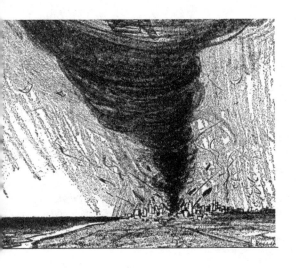

647 ➤ Batten down the hatches
At the time, the hurricane that struck Galveston, Texas, in 1900 was **the worst natural disaster in North American history** in terms of loss of life, estimated at six thousand to eight thousand deaths. The storm was measured as a category-four hurricane on a scale that goes up only to five.

648 ➤ What an opening
The Florida land boom got a hurricane hiccup in 1926 when a storm with 130-mile-an-hour winds crashed into the Atlantic coast. **Every building in the boom-town of Hollywood, Florida, was lost** except for the Masonic temple. The Great Miami Hurricane pushed the area into an early Depression and gave the University of Miami, which opened just days after the storm, a nickname for its sports teams—the Hurricanes.

649 ➤ Gone with the wind

A hurricane in 1634 **lifted up and blew away half the houses** in Massachusetts.

650 ➤ Snakes alive!

In 1928, a Caribbean hurricane struck the Lake Okeechobee area near West Palm Beach, Florida, killing some 2,500 people in the low-lying area. Desperate to escape the floodwaters, many people climbed trees—only to find the trees **full of deadly water moccasin snakes** that had also sought refuge. So many bodies were found floating in the Florida waterways that rescuers lashed them together in rafts of corpses that they towed behind their boats.

651 ➤ Look out below!

Something—probably an asteroid or comet, with a mass of at least 100,000 tons—struck Tunguska, Siberia, in 1908 with a force of ten to forty megatons of TNT. The blast, visible 435 kilometers away, incinerated 780 square kilometers of (thankfully) remote forest, and **herds of reindeer were reduced to ashes**.

652 ➤ Where's Superman when you need him?

Another cosmic crash almost destroyed the city of Pittsburgh in 1938. The half-million residents of the Steel City were surprised on June 24 by a bright light overhead, caused by a meteor, later **estimated at five hundred tons**, entering the atmosphere at a shallow angle. That angle caused the meteor and the subsequent explosion to miss the city, although the boom of impact rattled windows. Scientists said that if the meteor had descended at a more direct, straight-down angle, Pittsburgh would have been devastated.

653 ➤ But now we have a pool!

In September 1938, Long Island and New England got walloped by a hurricane that unexpectedly veered coastward instead of heading out to sea. Without warning, 186-mile-an-hour winds lashed Long Island, leaving only six houses still standing in Westhampton, and forty-foot tidal waves smashed the shoreline. Mansions in Newport, Rhode Island, washed away and guests at a posh seaside hotel **drowned when waves suddenly submerged the first-floor lounge and lobby**. Some five hundred people in all perished and nearly fourteen thousand structures were a total loss.

654 ➤ Cleveland rocked

One October day in 1944, a fifty-block section of Cleveland caught fire as liquid gas storage tanks owned by the East Ohio Gas Company mysteriously exploded. The blast shot flames high into the sky, gas mains ignited, and manhole covers blew off. Drivers trapped by the fire's advance **abandoned their cars and jumped into Lake Erie**. Ultimately, 3,600 people lost their homes and 135 died.

655 ➤ A burning river runs through it

The Cuyahoga River, which runs through Cleveland, has seen at least thirteen fires, dating to 1868, including a 1952 blaze that caused more than one million dollars in damage. A 1969 river fire helped spark the environmental movement when *Time* magazine described the polluted Cuyahoga as the **river that "oozes rather than flows" and in which a person "does not drown but decays."**

656 ➤ Breathing optional

In October 1954, heavy smog shut down the Los Angeles city's schools and most factories for the better part of the month. Some **drivers in the city's iconic convertibles wore gas masks**.

657 ➤ On a clear day you can see Pittsburgh

Los Angeles may be infamous for its smog, but the United States' first major casualties from smoggy air occurred in 1948 in Donora, Pennsylvania: **twenty people died, six hundred were hospitalized and thousands more were stricken**. The air didn't clear until rain washed the skies and the Donora Zinc Works temporarily shut down its smelters.

658 ➤ The smoggy streets of London town

The term "smog" was actually coined in 1905 in London, where this combination of smoke and fog would later turn deadly: **The Great Smog of 1952 enveloped the city, killing between two thousand and four thousand Londoners**. Many more filled the hospitals, gasping for breath because of low oxygen levels and suffocating amounts of pollution particulates.

659 ➤ Gotta build a bigger vacuum cleaner

Dust could also be disastrous, as the midsection of America found out during the Dust Bowl years of 1932 to 1937. Drought and unwise agricultural practices combined to turn the fertile prairies into a giant sandbox. When eighty-mile-an-hour winds roared through, "black blizzards" formed dusty storm fronts a thousand feet high and created **dirt drifts thirty feet deep**.

660 ⤳ More would've left if they could've seen the road

The Dust Bowl covered 300,000 square miles. **Half a million people would abandon their homes as they fled** the Dust Bowl and economic devastation in its wake.

661 ⤳ Grazing to the grave

Cows that ate dust-laden grass during the Dust Bowl years would later sicken and die from **"mud balls" that formed in their intestinal tract.**

662 ⤳ Brown lung

People, too, got sick from the omnipresent dust of 1932–1937. Many farmers simply **suffocated in their fields**, while others suffered later from "dust pneumonia."

663 ➤ Who turned out the lights?

During the height of the Dust Bowl, in 1934, clouds of dust blackened the daytime sky as far away as New York City. In Washington, D.C., **President Franklin D. Roosevelt found a film of prairie dust on his desk.**

664 ➤ Blowin' in the wind: most of Kansas

In two storms in May 1934, some 650 million tons of topsoil blew eastward off the plains in the nation's heartland. Experts estimated that **twelve million tons fell on Chicago** alone.

665 ➤ Chance of flurries and a bit colder

The Midwest had barely begun to recover from the Dust Bowl when, in 1941, a blizzard of the regular, snowy kind turned spring-like March weather suddenly deadly, claiming 151 lives. **Temperatures dropped fourteen degrees in only fifteen minutes** and eighty-five-mile-an-hour winds whipped snow into a whiteout. In North Dakota, one seventy-five-year-old man was found frozen to a telephone pole he'd grabbed against the wind, a mere fifty feet from the relative safety of his house. Two teenage girls, blinded by the blizzard, wandered onto the railroad tracks and were struck by a Northern Pacific locomotive—whose engineer didn't realize what had happened until he later found one of the girls' bodies frozen to the cowcatcher.

Acknowledgments

Although this book was drawn from hundreds of different sources, a few stand out as particularly useful and worthy of recommendation to readers interested in learning more about our often-horrifying history. These include:

➤ *At Home* by Bill Bryson, a splendidly rich social history

➤ *The Pessimist's Guide to History* by Doris Flexner and Stuart Berg Flexner, an essential guide to disasters of all sorts

➤ *The Good Old Days: They Were Terrible!*, a book filled with old photos published in 1974 by the famed archivist Otto Bettmann

➤ *The Straight Dope*, a newspaper column, also collected in book form and online, by Cecil Adams, whose answers to reader questions often illuminate terrifying truths about yesteryear

About the author

David A. Fryxell founded *Family Tree Magazine*, the nation's most popular genealogy publication, and continues to write for the magazine as a contributing editor and "History Matters" columnist. Formerly, Fryxell was also editorial director of *Writer's Digest Magazine* and wrote the magazine's Nonfiction column for more than a decade. He's the author of three books of writing instruction, *How to Write Fast (While Writing Well)*, *Elements of Article Writing: Structure and Flow*, and *Write Faster, Write Better*, as well as a book of humor, *Double-Parked on Main Street*. He's been an editor at *Pitt Magazine*, *TWA Ambassador*, *Horizon*, and *Milwaukee* magazines and the *St. Paul Pioneer Press* newspaper, and executive producer of Microsoft's Twin Cities Sidewalk website. He lives in Silver City, New Mexico, where he is editor and publisher of an award-winning regional monthly publication, *Desert Exposure* (www.desertexposure.com).

ISBN: 978-1-4403-2224-2

Other Family Tree Books are available from your local bookstore and online suppliers. For more genealogy resources, visit <shopfamilytree.com>.

16 15 14 13 12   5 4 3 2 1

DISTRIBUTED IN CANADA BY FRASER DIRECT
100 Armstrong Avenue
Georgetown, Ontario, Canada L7G 5S4
Tel: (905) 877-4411

media

DISTRIBUTED IN THE U.K. AND EUROPE BY
F&W Media International, LTD
Brunel House, Forde Close,
Newton Abbot, TQ12 4PU, UK
Tel: (+44) 1626 323200,
Fax: (+44) 1626 323319
E-mail: enquiries@fwmedia.com

PUBLISHER/EDITORIAL DIRECTOR: Allison Dolan

EDITOR: Jacqueline Musser

DESIGNER: Julie Barnett

PRODUCTION COORDINATOR: Debbie Thomas

DISTRIBUTED IN AUSTRALIA BY CAPRICORN LINK
P.O. Box 704, Windsor, NSW 2756 Australia
Tel: (02) 4577-3555

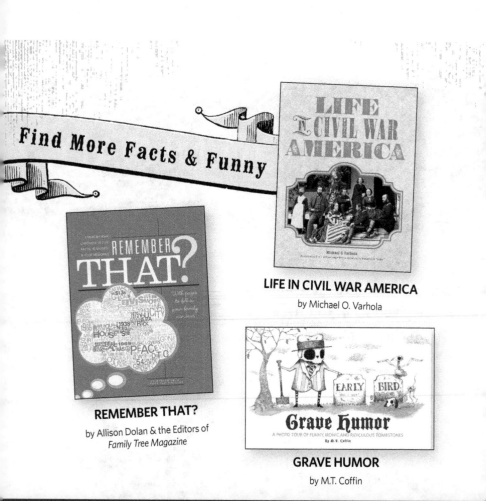

CPSIA information can be obtained
at www.ICGtesting.com
Printed in the USA
LVHW04s1914290818
588529LV00023B/299/P